VICTORIANS AT HOME

VICTORIANS AT HOME

Susan Lasdun

With an Introduction by Mark Girouard

WEIDENFELD & NICOLSON · LONDON

To Denys and my children

George Weidenfeld and Nicolson Limited
91 Clapham High Street
London SW4

ISBN 0 297 77942 7

Colour separations by Newsele Litho Ltd.
Filmset by Keyspools Ltd, Golborne, Warrington,
Lancs.

Printed and bound in Italy by
L.E.G.O. Vicenza

CONTENTS

PREFACE

This book is an attempt to chronicle the character of a range of English homes from the birth of Queen Victoria in 1819 to her death in 1901, and to understand this character in the light of the individuals who inhabited the homes. For this reason I have concentrated largely on homes whose owners' tastes and life-styles can be firmly established from surviving diaries and other documents, and more importantly, where the contemporary interiors have been recorded in drawings or photographs. For the sake of simplicity, however, I have used the term Victorian in the title to apply to the period covered not only by Queen Victoria's reign but by her entire life.

I am greatly indebted to all the private owners and custodians of public collections who made available to me both written and visual records, and in many cases gave up their time as well. Details of sources are given in the Notes at the end of the book.

I would like to thank all those who gave me the benefit of their scholarship, in particular, Geoffrey de Bellaigue, Mary Burkett, John Christian, Nicholas Cooper, David Dean, John Hardy, Joan Langton, Jill Lever, Sir Oliver Millar, Margaret Richardson, Victoria Slowe, John T. Smith, Lindsay Stainton, Peter Thornton, Clive Wainwright, Dennis Cole and Gordon Rattray Taylor.

I owe thanks to Mark Boxer, Lord Briggs and Mark Girouard for their encouragement to write the book, to Sarah Strong and Eileen Harris who lent me their manuscripts, to John Cornforth, Dorothy Girouard and John Nicoll for their help, to Sally Newton for typing it, to Sara Komar for her elegant design, and to my editor Martha Caute for her patience and skill.

SUSAN LASDUN

INTRODUCTION

It is rather too easy to think of the Victorian age as a kind of museum exhibit, divided into neatly definable sections, each with its own characteristics. Whereas, like any age, it is more in the nature of a mosaic, made up of hundreds of thousands of different pieces. More of one kind of piece occur in one section than another, and as a result certain patterns emerge about which one can make generalizations; but the variety of the individual pieces is endless, each section is a medley of contrasts, and pieces with characteristics generally thought of as typical of one period have a disconcerting way of turning up in another.

The pieces of the mosaic include innumerable family households, each with its own unique but constantly changing identity, each inheriting certain attitudes, and often objects and homes to go with them, but also acquiring new ones, picking up new fashions, moving up in the social scale and changing its life-style accordingly. The variety is endless, and this book tries to give some impression of it by looking at the settings which a number of families and family groups created for themselves. It includes among others the houses of Queen Victoria, her mother, her son, two bankers, a group of Whig grandees, a bachelor museum curator, an Irish absentee landlord, a painter, a schoolmaster, an engineer, a cement manufacturer, and a Church of England canon. It ranges, in fact, from the grandest in the land to the mid-middle classes; on the whole it was only within that range that families had the means or the desire to record the settings in which they lived. Comprehensive records of the interiors of Victorian cottages, farmhouses and tenements are hard, if not impossible, to find, but a scattering of individual views survive, and a section of these is included.

It is something of a shock to realize that such homes existed side by side with the other interiors illustrated in this book. Even the farmhouse (p. 147) seems to come from a different world; while the poorer cottage interiors vividly epitomize the great substratum of poverty on which Victorian middle- and upper-class comfort rested, and to a considerable extent depended. But even within what one might call the zone of comfort there are fascinating contrasts of character, and survivals out of context. In about 1880 the artist G.A.Storey was eating in a St John's Wood dining-room (p. 110) which one would confidently date thirty or forty years earlier, were it not for the light-fitting. At much the same period the Prince and

Princess of Wales, and Edward and Georgiana Burne-Jones were living in houses which, although geographically only a few miles from each other, seem worlds apart in character; and yet each was, in its very different way, typical of two totally different aspects of later Victorian society – the richly Philistine and discriminatingly artistic.

One of the pay-offs of dealing with houses in terms of families is that one gets to know the families – something that is obviously impossible when interiors are dealt with purely in chronological and art-historical sequence. Inevitably, some families are more obviously expressed by the rooms in which they live than others, and interiors in which people are shown as well as contents tend to tell one more than ones in which they are not. Few readers of this book will, one suspects, fail to be delighted by the Drummonds as depicted in the enchanting pictures drawn by the children of the family.

Here again preconceptions are usefully upset. One expects the children to be rigidly disciplined, and in a sense they are. The birch and the backboard are drawn with a fascinated sense of drama by the child artists. But the general atmosphere is not at all strict or rigid. Children and adults, far from being kept separate, do everything together: the girls and boys, apart from playing hide-and-seek on their own, watch their mother at her dressing-table and what appear to be jolly uncles cock-fighting on the hearth-rug, and are even present at the wonderfully stiff business of receiving morning calls. Somehow the disciplined but relaxed life seems admirably suited to the high-ceilinged but uncluttered rooms and the tall sash windows, opened to their full extent so that the fresh air can flood in from the Buckinghamshire landscape outside.

Another endearing character vividly portrayed by his own drawings is George Scharf, the first Director of the National Portrait Gallery. It was an extraordinary piece of good fortune that this industrious bachelor should have set to work in 1868–9 and meticulously and accurately depicted his rooms in Westminster apparently exactly as they were, with no attempt to tidy or rearrange; and moreover that he should also have kept a diary as meticulous as the drawings. And so one finds oneself carried into a particular stream of scholarly bachelor clutter which lasted on until a decade or two ago in the rooms of old-fashioned Cambridge and Oxford dons. Books are stacked and piled everywhere; pictures, busts and casts of classical sculpture jostle against the solid, totally unpretentious furniture, and spill over into the bedroom, where the casts gaze in wild profusion at the jacket hanging on the door, the hairbrushes on the dressing-table and the hip-bath in front of the fireplace. Scharf is not present himself, but his 'most preferred friend' Jack Pattisson is, and so is his old mother, tucked away upstairs looking over the roof-tops of Westminster, and patiently (one hopes) enduring being surrounded by what appear to be her

Members of the Harden family sewing at Brathay Hall in the Lake District; drawing by John Harden, 1804–5.

son's possessions rather than her own.

Scharf's drawings give one a vivid feeling of having been transported back through time and actually being in the room oneself. This quality of pulling one into a room is rare in drawings, and, curiously enough, even rarer in photographs, impossible though it may be for the camera to lie. Some have it, however, for instance the photographs in this book of Thomas Summerson's house, especially that of the entrance hall (p. 135), looking at which one can almost smell the damp overcoats – just as, looking at some of John Harden's wonderful drawings of his family life in the Lake District, one can almost hear the music. The Harden drawings do more than vividly recreate the life of a family: they epitomize the life-style (or rather, one of the life-styles) of an epoch. The whole of Jane Austen seems encapsulated, for instance, in one little drawing (slightly earlier than most in the series) of a group of Harden ladies seated round a table at their sewing. Implicit in it is a world of elegantly tinkling music and elegantly tapering tables, of people of moderate but comfortable incomes living pleasantly and sociably together, making music, playing cards, delicately embroidering, in the clear light of high-ceilinged rooms. Nothing is ponderous; the furniture is as delicate as the music and can be carried easily round the room to catch the light at a window or the heat of a fire.

It is intriguing to compare this drawing with a photograph of a similar scene at Pitfour in Scotland, taken perhaps forty or fifty years later. A group of ladies is sitting round a table near a window, but the life-style has entirely changed. Everything is comfortably patterned, padded and puffed out; the table legs have swollen and so have the skirts of the ladies. Stylishness has been replaced by cosiness.

It is tempting to see this as the difference between late-Georgian and mid-Victorian life-styles. But it is not quite as simple as that. For more or less concurrently with the elegant, sparsely furnished and on occasion even bare-boarded rooms of the Hardens, George IV and the aristocracy of his day were evolving a quite different style of interior, the opulent and elaborate style of the rooms at Windsor Castle and Buckingham Palace. Here one can find Victorian plushness and clutter in embryo – and not as embryonic as all that. But it is fascinating to see that the young Victoria reacted away from it, and that when she escaped from her official residence to her new private retreats at Osborne and Balmoral, the settings which she and Prince Albert devised for their personal use were much closer to the world of the Hardens than of George IV. Her bedrooms at Osborne and Balmoral may not have the especial elegance of the early nineteenth century, and they use patterns much more abundantly; but they are none the less remarkably stylish in an unassuming way. Victoria liked to think that the result was cosy (a favourite adjective of hers), but it was also entirely without padding or clutter. The use of tartan at Balmoral, about which endless jokes have been made, is in fact brilliantly creative.

Clutter, however, was on the way in royal circles, and an over-abundance of cosiness with it. They were to be all too apparent in Victoria's rooms in her old age, as in the rooms of her son and daughter-in-law at Marlborough House. A similar mixture, even if not quite so concentrated, is equally in evidence in the

A group of ladies in the back drawing-room of a house at Pitfour in Scotland, c. 1855.

11

aristocratic interiors of Broadlands, Brocket and Panshanger, as rearranged in the mid-nineteenth century, and in the Duchess of Marlborough's boudoir; the latter hilariously suggests that the Duchess had been unexpectedly moved out of a villa in Peckham into the Vanbrughian splendours of Blenheim. The almost total lack of visual discrimination which the arrangement of all these rooms shows demonstrates how whole-heartedly the aristocracy and the Royal Family were addicted to what some might think of as middle-class tastelessness. Any sense of style is completely absent.

It is, of course, unfair to generalize about the upper classes on the strength of a few drawings and photographs. But in fact plenty more evidence exists to support this belief. There were many exceptions, but on the whole a sense of style in architecture and decoration was not a characteristic of the upper classes in the second half of the nineteenth century. Even those who had it were seldom innovators. The initiative had passed to the middle classes. The upper classes were looking for what, on the whole, they have been looking for ever since: a relaxed comfort that was trying so hard not to look too forced or arranged that it tended to become entirely shapeless. The contrast to the exquisite interiors devised for the aristocracy in the eighteenth century was total.

It was the middle classes who now had a sense of style. By no means all of them had it, of course, and sometimes the style was heavily shot with osten-tation. Mrs Samuel and her children in their wildly pseudo-Japanese boudoir in Bayswater (as depicted on p. 109 in one of the most splendid pictures in the book) have rather too obviously surrendered themselves to a smart decorator not quite out of the top drawer. One can imagine what fun those of the aristocracy who penetrated it would have made of its *nouveau-riche* display. And yet the Samuels were more in the tradition of Kent and Adam than the Cowpers and Palmerstons. Similarly, the mildly Art Nouveau décor of the cement-manufacturing Brookses shows impressive discrimination for a middle-class family in an outer suburb of London; the cotton-spinning Coateses from Glasgow went to one of the more original designers of the late nineteenth century when they were doing up their home near Birmingham. Neither of these houses has the relaxed quality of the Palmerston circle; perhaps a feature of the Victorians was that a sense of style and a sense of ease tended to part company. But James Kitson, the Leeds engine manufacturer, enjoyed both stylishness and comfort in the discreetly opulent interiors which were created for him inside his Palladian house on the outskirts of Leeds.

Kitson was the proud possessor of Millais's painting *Forget-me-not*; and to judge from surviving photographs, Millais's own handsome London house in

The Duchess of Marlborough in her boudoir at Blenheim Palace; drawing by George Scharf, 1864.

The Duchess of Marlborough's Boudoir, Blenheim Palace —

dark green

crimson

green

Duchess of
Marlborough

green.
given to Lord Randolph Churchill for his birthday
February 13th 1864.

brown

steel

GD. Blenheim. Feb January. 1864.

Prince's Gate had something of the same character. The interiors which the Burne-Joneses created inside their rambling eighteenth-century house in Fulham were entirely different; they were at the other end of the Victorian artistic spectrum, in a semi-magical world of rich colours and patterns, exotic pottery and pictures crowded with angels, gods, knights and monsters. All this was threaded through with a curiously homespun element; although comfort was not entirely lacking, it was certainly not at a premium. In spite of numerous modifications, one can see how the resulting mixture influenced the settings which the Bloomsbury group created for themselves in the 1920s.

Burne-Jones, like his friend William Morris, loathed the typical interior décor of his own day. Yet it is a curious aspect of almost any period that rooms which are deliberately different cannot help being in some ways the same. Take, for instance, the drawing-room of the house of an unidentified Scottish merchant living at Leith, as photographed in about 1890. Burne-Jones would almost certainly have found the house insufferably bourgeois; and yet its rich gloom is recognizably related to the rich Burne-Jones twilight, although one is created by Morris wallpaper and Burne-Jones's own pictures and stained-glass windows, and the other is dependent on

The drawing-room of an unidentified Scottish house, probably at Leith, c. 1890.

whole-hearted abandon to potted plants, bronzes, and what the Russians still call 'ploosh'.

Light in houses is a fascinating subject of study. The mid-Victorians kept it out, the early and late Victorians let it in. Why was this? It is tempting to look for practical reasons. Light is essential for embroidery and for reading. The window shown in the drawing of the Hardens sewing has no curtains at all; light comes freely through onto the table where the ladies are at work. Doing 'useful work' with the needle was considered a necessary quality of a gentlewoman in the early nineteenth century. By High Victorian times having a wife who did nothing except make empty conversation during morning calls had become a status symbol; there was money enough to buy freely in the shops, and plenty of servants to do all the work. So the windows retreated behind layers of rich stuffs, the light dwindled, and the women sat idly but richly in the gloom.

The theory, however, even if it might correspond to actual situations in one or two cases, really does not work. The ladies in the circle of Morris and Burne-Jones embroidered as fervently as the Harden ladies, if not more so; and yet they lived on the whole in gloom, or at least in much less light than the generation before them; and Art Nouveau ladies around 1900 inhabited shiny white interiors, and often did not embroider at all. Both light and whiteness at this period had something to do with a new enthusiasm for hygiene; and yet one suspects this

ABOVE *A formidable group in the conservatory at Bishopsgate, near Egham, Surrey, c. 1910.*

was only part of the story. Gloom was romantic, light a symbol of progress; practical aspects are important in discussing interiors, but they are not everything.

Were conservatories practical or were they romantic? They had certain practical properties: they were useful for sitting out in during dances; they provided pot plants for the house conveniently to hand; in

RIGHT *The Harden family at Brathay Hall, 1827. John Harden's watercolour captures the ease with which the different generations and sexes among his family pursued their various interests together. It also contains a rare sketch of a hinged sun-blind of pleated silk fitted to the inside of the window through which, when the blind was closed, a green light filtered, thought to be 'very comfortable to the sight'. This blind was a development of a 'sash' – a sun-blind introduced in the seventeenth century.*

winter they kept summer going, as it were, in at least one little corner of the house. And no doubt conservatories were also a status symbol: the size of the conservatory and the richness and rareness of its contents was one way of displaying the prosperity of its owner. They had another, not on the face of it obvious, use demonstrated by the wonderful (Edwardian) group in the conservatory at Bishopsgate near Egham: they enabled people to be photographed in comfortable and well lit conditions in the depths of winter. But they were also surely romantic, or in part romantic; they were magically rich and sweet-scented bowers of colour and greenery that carried a touch of the jungle and the tropics into English suburbs and English winters.

The interplay between practical and symbolic or emotional needs is always intriguing. One very often works against the other (usually the symbolic and emotional against the practical); perhaps the most sympathetic interiors are those where the two are in

A bedroom in a town house; watercolour by Samuel Rayner, c. 1855. The dressing-table, with its ritual cloths, candles and smaller companion table, is strongly reminiscent of an altar and its serving table. The main bedroom of the house, known then as now as the master bedroom, has always been essentially a feminine room as this drawing demonstrates. The wash-stand in the corner was common to all middle- and upper-class Victorian bedrooms. (See also pp. 57–8.)

perfect accord. There clearly have to be chairs to sit on, tables to eat or work on, shelves for books, walls and ceilings to shelter, fires or substitutes for fires to warm, lamps and windows to light. Comfort suggests curtains to control the light, upholstery to pad out the chairs, carpets to soften the floors and reduce the noise level. A practical feature which figures in many Victorian interiors is a generously sized (usually round) table, situated for warmth or light by the fire or window, or under the gas lamps, round which the ladies sat to work at embroidery, drawing or illumination, or even to read books. (The tradition that the normal way to read a book was sitting at a table only gradually died in the nineteenth century.)

But such practical elements tend to disappear beneath less practical ones, at no time more so than in the nineteenth century. The desire to display objects of no practical use went to much further lengths in the period than it had ever done before. Rich people in the eighteenth century had bought pictures and collected china, and used their rooms to display them, and so, to a limited degree, had prosperous members of the middle classes. But now more and more people were collecting more and more objects, partly because there was more money all round, partly because large numbers of mass-produced, decorative objects were available at comparatively little expense, partly because collecting something or other became, in the nineteenth century, a widespread craze, not just one confined to a few dilettanti. As a result, it is worth noting that nearly all the interiors illustrated in this book are furnished abundantly and in some cases over-abundantly with decorative objects, something which was much less likely to be the case in the eighteenth (and still less in the seventeenth) century. The only exceptions are one or two of the Harden interiors, the earliest in the book, and Thomas Summerson's bedroom (p. 135). The latter is interesting because Summerson was a self-made man who started from very humble origins, and the furnishing of his bedroom probably represented his own personal taste acquired from what he had been used to in childhood; whereas the rest of the house, photographed shortly after his death in 1898, reflects the more affluent taste of his children. Of course, the cottage interiors are a very different matter from everything else in the book: they have no soft furnishings and little of anything in the way of ornament. It is part of the appalling gap between 'haves' and 'have-nots' in Victorian society, which however much one can conceive of it intellectually, still gives one a feeling of shock when one sees it presented visually (although it is no greater than the gap between the Western and the Third World today).

But the accumulation of objects can, of course, take many forms. What objects were to be accumulated, and how were they to be arranged? Certain symbolic images do tend to present themselves when one is looking at Victorian rooms. Some are naturalistic ones: the image of a cave, a forest, a nest. Most Victorians were incurable nest-makers; but their equivalents of twigs, straw, and leaves were Japanese fans, vases, photographs, bronze statues, and clocks, which they wove together into a richly indistinguishable fuzz. Burne-Jones, on the other hand, created a forest, lined with the leaves and foliage of Morris wallpaper and embroideries, and filled with mysterious light percolating through hangings and stained-glass windows. Other interiors combined elements of both nest and forest, the forest being almost literally provided by the potted palms and other greenery which spilled over from the conservatory into all the living rooms of the more prosperous Victorian homes. Both nests and forests suggest an element of escapism, just as the accumulation of objects suggests a desire for security. They probably do so with reason. It is so easy to think of the Victorian as a smug and self-confident age, but one only has to make a very superficial dip into Victorian letters and literature to see how far this was from being the case: doubt, despair, fear of revolution, dislike of the way the world was changing round them, mystification and worry at what science was up to, are all too apparent.

But other images and impulses are in evidence, in addition to these basic ones. One is the desire to be in the fashion: the Japanese craze, which transformed Mrs Samuel's boudoir and the last wash of which landed a solitary Japanese fan in one room of the cement-manufacturing Brookses, seems to have swept the land independently of any desire of those who participated in it to see themselves as geisha girls or Samurai warriors. There was, however, often an element of self-identification in the stylistic games which figure so prominently in some interiors. Various varieties of rococo or Louis XIV revival, for instance, seem to show a deliberate desire to identify with an aristocratic or elegant society of the past; gentlemen in Moorish smoking-rooms dreamed of harems.

Revivals in the nineteenth century did not come round as quickly as nowadays, when the fashions of twenty or thirty years ago have a way of reappearing. But it is interesting to see that Canon Valpy in the late 1890s is clearly reacting against mid-Victorian cosiness and nest-building and going back to the spare and spindly elegance of families like the Hardens; only his interiors are not *quite* so spare and spindly, and Victorian experiments in comfort have left a residue of chintz-covered armchairs and sofas such as the Hardens never aspired to. The result is delightful in its air of delicate and civilized comfort.

Another quite different image was that of the farmhouse or cottage. A certain type of middle-class Victorian liked to think of himself as a sturdy yeoman, uncorrupted by aristocratic nonsense, and a rustic element in tables, chairs and other furniture, and in ingle-nooks and door-latches, was a result. One can see it at work, combined with much that has nothing to do with farmhouses or cottages, in the sturdy table and Windsor chairs of Burne-Jones's dining-room, and in almost every room of the Glaswegian Coateses. It helped produce those stiff-backed chairs and settles which are typical of a certain type of late Victorian middle-class house, and are usually as uncomfortable as they look.

Such rustic echoes may have suggested disapproval of, or at least independence from, the aristocracy but they rarely worked the other way so as to involve breaking the barriers between masters and servants. The very limited extent to which servants and the rooms in which they lived and worked feature in this book is not just an accident of selection; it corresponds to a real situation. There were, of course and invariably, exceptions; but the barrier between employers and servants in the Victorian age was more rigid than it had ever been. The exceptions in this book are significant. Apart from the intensely evocative view of Thomas Summerson's larder (p. 135, the only photograph of a Victorian larder that I know of) they are confined to the beginning of the period. John Harden made an exquisite watercolour study of his scullery maid at work in her scullery (p. 31). In the Drummond pictures servants figure constantly both at work in the rooms and in delightfully naïve individual portraits. This is the second earliest group of drawings in the book, but still more significantly the pictures are drawn by children who always tended to have a closer personal

relationship with servants than their parents, and moreover did not yet realize that servants occupied a different and inferior status; everyone was a human being to them.

Servants were probably just as much, if not more, exploited in the eighteenth century than the nineteenth, but the tendency to treat them as though they did not exist was a specifically nineteenth-century one. It is perhaps significant that in 1846 George Scharf's father, George Scharf Senior, made a delightful drawing of his own kitchen with the cook in

George Scharf Senior's drawing of his kitchen in Francis Street, London, 1846.

it; but his son, drawing the rooms in which he and his mother and aunt lived literally inch by inch in 1868–9, excluded his servants entirely. His diary reveals the existence of the couple who looked after him, Mr and Mrs Lee, and of a maid who had to be sacked because she brought a man in to spend the night with her; but dearly as one would like to know as much about this aspect of his life as about the rest of it, his drawings ignore both servants' rooms and servants. Similarly Charlotte Bosanquet's drawings, intensely evocative as they are of the country-house round of a prosperous early Victorian spinster, never feature the servants.

George Scharf Senior's kitchen comes, in fact, much closer to a genuine farmhouse kitchen-cum-living-room than the pseudo-farmhouse rooms that began to appear 'upstairs' rather than 'downstairs' at the end of the century. In many ways the farmhouse kitchen is clearly much less comfortable than the 'upstairs' rooms; but the great kitchen ranges or open fire-places probably made them considerably warmer. Photographs and illustrations of Victorian rooms may suggest a warm nest, but one must remember that, however nest-like, they were seldom very warm. One of the many fascinating sidelights which Susan Lasdun brings up to intrigue one with is that even Queen Victoria was often so bitterly cold at Windsor that she had to tramp up and down the great Corridor in an effort to get the circulation going – using it, in fact, as the Elizabethans had their long galleries.

In spite of all the differences in decoration, life-style and income of the houses in this book, they all have one feature – or rather the lack of one feature – in common: none of them appear to have any form of central heating. The stove in a room of the cement-manufacturing Brookses (p. 132) is the only departure from an open coal fire in the whole book. There were, of course, houses with central heating in the nineteenth century, but the lack of them in the book is not accidental. Central heating was only adopted by a minority, and the majority tended to think of it as un-English and unhealthy. Of course the invisible servants were there, to stoke up coal fires all over the house; but even so, as Americans and Europeans constantly pointed out, English houses were un-bearably cold, and most of them remained so far into this century.

On the whole domestic technology was unremark-able in the nineteenth century; labour was so cheap that there was comparatively little pressure for change. The Prince of Wales, had no less than 120 servants at Marlborough House (admittedly includ-ing outdoor servants); at the other end of the scale the Summerson household, the least assuming of the middle-class homes featured in this book, is unlikely to have had less than two or three, although the exact number does not seem to be documented. The superb bathroom (p. 142) for the Kitson house outside Leeds, lustrous with Burmantoft tiles from floor to ceiling, was designed *c.* 1885 but was essentially a foretaste of the Edwardian age. Many Victorian households did without a bathroom altogether – even, occasionally, very grand ones. George Scharf, Susan Lasdun reveals, used to take his bath in the local public baths, until he invested in a hip-bath in 1864; it is one of the numerous curious and enlightening nuggets of information with which her book regales us.

MARK GIROUARD

JOHN HARDEN

John Harden, born in 1772, was a gentleman by virtue of the lands which he owned in Ireland. Comfortably off but not rich, he had little inclination to go into business, choosing rather to become an amateur artist. He painted in the tradition of the landscape painters of his time and not surprisingly preferred rural surroundings to those of the city. There was the added advantage that with life in the country being cheaper than in the city, he could maintain a higher standard of living.

In 1804, one year after his marriage to Jessy Allan, whose family lived in Edinburgh, he took his mother, wife and baby son to live in the Lake District, already a haunt for poets, painters and travellers. A friend who had been charged to find them a house rented one for them half a mile outside Ambleside. It was situated like 'a white palace at the head of Wynandemere', and was, as Jessy wrote to her sister Agnes in India, 'the best one in Windemere'. Built in

Piano and chess, 1826. John Harden's watercolours portray the informal yet busy domestic life of his family and friends. The early piano shows a great similarity to the harpsichord from which pianos were derived. A canterbury, to hold music, fits under the piano.

1788, it was a square, three-storied stone house, with two one-storey wings flanking either side. The house was called Brathay Hall and is still standing today.

The Hardens lived at Brathay Hall for thirty years and brought up three sons and two daughters there. The poet Robert Southey, a neighbour and friend of the Hardens, wrote in his collection of fictional letters about the English that: 'There are two words in their language which these people pride themselves on. . . . Home is the one. . . . The other word is comfort.' In this sense, the Hardens were an archetypal English family. Their domesticity is recorded in hundreds of drawings by John Harden. Complementing his drawings are the Journals which Jessy wrote in the form of long letters to her sister Agnes in India. When Agnes returned to England in 1812 the Journals ceased, but John Harden's drawings continued.

The Journals disclose the Hardens' absorption in the daily minutiae of their lives to the almost total exclusion of the outside world. Occasional comments on the extravagances of the Royal Family or misdemeanours in high society were related to Agnes, while other external events were only noted if they touched on the life of someone in their circle, such as the death of Captain Wordsworth when the ss *Abergavenny* sank. He was the brother of their friends

Dorothy and William Wordsworth who were living close by. The same remoteness from public issues can be seen in the novels of Jane Austen, where reference to the Napoleonic Wars is limited to the attraction of scarlet-coated soldiers for her heroines.

The key to the Hardens' lives was the leisure that they enjoyed. In the summer this was spent in entertaining 'a concourse of visitors and ramblers' with boating parties, bathing, fishing, picnics and excursions in the 'jaunting carr' – 'guiding and accompanying my friends from one beauty to another', related John Harden in a postscript to one of his wife's letters. At the end of the day there was 6 o'clock tea to which their neighbours might come and be diverted with an impromptu 'hop to the piano'. 'The gaiety of this place is wonderful, think of us having 25 people on Monday and 18 last night, all different yet this is thought to be a retired place.' Harden was as happy 'charioteering' his guests as painting his pictures. There was plenty of time for that, and both he and Jessy, who had had drawing lessons in Edinburgh with the Scottish painter, Alexander Nasmyth, went off sketching together, sometimes joined by other artists such as John Constable and Richard Shannon.

The Hardens were just as happy in winter when for four or five months it was all 'quiet and repose'. The eighteenth-century ideal of the cultivation of the 'polite arts' stood them in good stead when they were thrown upon their own resources. Bad weather which kept them indoors was actually welcomed by Jessy, not only because she was 'so fond of the house', but also because it gave her leisure to follow the occupations she most liked. These were painting and music-making, which sometimes took the form of whole mornings or 'forenoons' playing duets with her mother-in-law; sometimes she accompanied her husband's flute or sang glees when enough voices were assembled. Much time was also spent reading novels or weightier works like the eight volumes of Tacitus. When Jessy's father and sister were staying, the evenings were passed playing cards or at the piano, or the women listened to the men reading whilst sitting at their 'work'. 'Our family party is so well consti-tuted that we amuse each other very well,' wrote John Harden to Agnes. Their relaxed enjoyment of their life and of each other was rare and quite disarming.

They had the same easy-going attitude to church. If the weather was bad on a Sunday, John Harden read a sermon at home for the family and the servants. At times he disregarded Sunday com-

Music and reading, 1827. John Harden's wife Jessy, distinguished from the younger generation by her bonnet, is dressed like them in white muslin or lawn, a fashion since the Napoleonic Wars when material other than cotton became scarce. In the 1820s women still favoured white for morning wear. The gentleman's funereal black coat and trousers signalled the future trend in men's clothing.

Playing the flute, c. 1820. The readers show admirable powers of concentration as their friend makes music on his flute. The light-weight furniture, including the portable writing-desk on a small tripod table, is designed to be easily rearranged to suit different activities and times of day.

pletely, going off to paint instead. Jessy, with her Presbyterian background, was critical of this, though reasoned that painting on Sunday was surely better than 'idle chatter' which was the common way of passing the day. Their daughters Jessie and Jane, in contrast, reflected the increasing evangelicalism of their age and were consciously pious and soul-searching. Jessie's diary reveals her preoccupation with the improvement of the soul in such entries as 'I grieve to say my temper has this evening been bad, Satan is always ready to attack us when we are off our guard'; she also tells of leaving tracts in the village or examining the children in Sunday school on their Catechism.

In keeping with their independence the Hardens arranged their meal-times entirely to suit themselves. In 1808 Jessy told her mother: 'We breakfast now at 8 o'clock, dine at 4, drink tea at 6 and sup at half past 9, but remember we don't go to bed until 11 o'clock, for I work and John reads after supper our reason for putting off the dinner hour is that we may have a long morning.' Soon, in more fashionable circles, dinner was being served much later; the hunger pangs that that created were satiated by luncheon. In 1818, Lord Landsdowne in his house at Bowood in Wiltshire served luncheon regularly between 1.00 and 2.00 p.m., yet in 1842 young Jessie Harden was still dining at 4.00 p.m. It was many years before meal-times were stabilized even among the upper classes. Suffice it to say that the main meal of the day was generally called dinner, a distinction which has remained in most classes irrespective of the hour at which it is eaten.

Though the tenor of their lives was remarkably carefree, there was one sorrow common to many families until the present century which the Hardens shared. This was the death of a child in infancy. Jessy had one stillborn baby and one who died when only a few weeks old.

One of the characteristics of their life – which John Harden's drawings demonstrate – was that not only did the two sexes pass their time together, but also the different generations shared the same occupations. The tendency of Victorians to separate the sexes and ages into different domains, a trait which increased as the century progressed, was delightfully absent from the Harden household. Jessy and her mother-in-law taught the children to read before they started to go to school, while Harden professed that he preferred to play with his son Allan than to go fishing. The Hardens' letters are full of 'Dear, darling Allan . . . is the sweetest little cherub', or 'darling Jovy', or 'dear Jane Sophia . . . the dear child comes on wonderfully'. There was an informality in their relationships with their children that was lacking in the authoritarianism which, ironically, their children's generation often adopted when they became parents themselves.

The Hardens' informality extended to their relationships with their neighbours although, if they were too grand, thus involving their hosts in great

Old Mrs Harden, 1824. John Harden's mother is seated on an eighteenth-century chair encased in a slip-cover, intended perhaps to give added warmth as well as to protect the upholstery.

expense, they were not cultivated. A Mrs Pritchard was found 'too ceremonious and stylish', and so were the Briglands who arrived to stay with a maid, footman, coachman and four horses. Jessy wrote that they were 'no joke to entertain'.

'The only plague I have in life is servants,' Jessy complained to Agnes. 'They are in the first place very extravagant in wages . . . we are obliged to keep no less than 5 . . . the gardener has 24 guineas, the footman 10 and *clothes*, which you may reckon 10 more; the cook 10, nursery maid $8\frac{1}{2}$ and housemaid 6.' Their total wages came to £68 a year which was only £8 more than Emily Kitson was paying her father's butler at Gledhow Hall eighty years later (see p. 142). Apart

from the 'great expence' of their salaries, Jessy found the servants so 'high' that if she found fault with them they simply walked out. In later years extra housemaids were employed and Jessy mentions a nanny in her letters. They also added a dairymaid and three more men for the grounds. They rented forty acres of land, kept a few cows and grew all their vegetables. The house, garden and land were let to them at first on a nine-year lease for only £85 a year, in addition to which they had to pay taxes of £20. Jessy reckoned on £1,000 being a necessary annual income for such a life-style.

When the Hardens rented Brathay it was furnished with standing furniture and 'excellent beds'. A year later their landlord sold the furniture, some of which they probably bought. They were also obliged to purchase more and spent £30 at Ulverston, which did not, however, go very far. The rest came from a two-day sale at a house in Rydal where they spent another £40 on the first day, and on the second day bought 'a dozen mahogany chairs at a guinea each, and a dozen rush bottom bedroom ones at 5s 4d'. Jessy thought that some things were probably as dear as if bought new. 'The best bargain of all is a very good set of blue tableware, complete, tho' rather short at $3\frac{1}{2}$ gns.'

This then was the furniture that Harden meticulously drew. The most striking feature which his drawings reveal is the lack of formal arrangement of the furniture when in use. The Hardens obviously moved it around to be close to the fire or near the light, which in the evenings consisted only of a couple of candles. Most homes of people of their standing would have had oil-lamps as well as candles, yet there are none shown in Harden's drawings. It is worth noting that in 1823 Walter Scott was installing gaslight in his home at Abbotsford. The Harden furniture was either late eighteenth-century or early nineteenth-century. It reflected the wide variety of different pieces that were available at the time, while its lightness was a result of the need for furniture to be portable. There were little nests of tables, portable table desks, round pedestal tables, small Pembroke tables, delicate work tables, tripod tables, shield-back Hepplewhite-style chairs and many other pieces. They were light enough to be trundled in front of the hearth – a fact that signified to Lord Torrington, writing in the late eighteenth century, a total failure to warm a house adequately.

I love large, firmly fix'd writing tables in my library; and to have my breakfast, and dining tables substantial, and immoveable: and when I say immoveable, it is because my rooms, and every part of them, should be of an equal warmth; and there should be no need, as I see at present, of little scuttling tables being brought before the hearth. In my house ... I should desire that none would come within six feet of the fireplace; nor would anyone wish it, because the grates would be ample, and the fireplace high and extended; not a little low dug hole, as at present, surrounded by a slip of marble. . . .

Scullery maid, 1820–30. The scullery is full of traditional objects such as the table and trestle-bench, the all-purpose swill basket (on the right), the swill or osier basket with a handle beneath the sink, the wooden cooper, the cast-iron cooking pots some of which are designed to hang on a chimney-crane over the fire, and the lantern or lanthorn made at the local horn works in Kendal.

The fireplaces at Brathay were not the little dug holes deplored by Lord Torrington, but had been designed according to the principles of the most notable reformer in domestic heating and cooking arrangements at the time, the American Count Rumford. He recommended narrowing the throat of the chimney and reducing the width of the fireplace by building two inclined surrounds on either side of the opening. Though this greatly increased the efficiency of the fire, it still did not dispense with the need to crowd around the hearth. Although the Hardens' house remained deficient in its heating

OPPOSITE AND ABOVE *Family and friends, 1824–6. Some of Count Rumford's improvements in fireplace design can be seen in the drawing above: the narrowing of the opening, the inclined surrounds and the basket grate placed in a niche. Nevertheless, the need to crowd round the hearth persisted. The adjustable pole-screen in the drawing opposite was to give protection from the heat at close quarters.*

arrangements, it was nevertheless, like their neighbour Wordsworth's, an example of a home 'where comfort and culture were secured without display'.

THE DRUMMOND FAMILY

The early nineteenth century was not only an age for 'improving' houses but also for 'improving' people. The Drummond children's drawings depict the story of their own 'improvement' within their family home. It was the home of a well-to-do, well-connected family – indeed 'one of the noblest Scottish families'.

The children's great-great-grandfather founded, in 1717, Drummond's Bank in Charing Cross. Their father Andrew became a partner in the bank in 1818 when it became clear that he would not follow in the footsteps of his elder reprobate brother George, who nearly gambled the Drummond fortune away and sold the family home at Stanmore to pay his debts. Andrew Drummond married Lady Emily Charlotte Percy, daughter of the Earl of Beverley. Their children, one son and six daughters, grew up at The Tile House in Denham, Buckinghamshire, close to where their cousins lived, one of whom was Fanny Drummond. Fanny's poems, letters and essays, transcribed into an album belonging to her mother, were about the children's upbringing and the duties of governesses. This album and the drawings by her cousins of scenes in their childhood reveal the principles which guided the Drummonds' family life. The guileless charm of the pictures provides a lively illustration of pleasure, punishment and pain. They show a family which seems to be striving to reconcile the pleasures and tastes of the fashionable world with the strictures of the severest moralists; modishly-dressed adults administering backboards and birch-rods to crying children on the one hand, and joining them in delightful party games on the other, reveal the contrasting aspects of their family life.

The drawings are a reminder that this was a period when the supremacy of the 'polite arts' was being challenged by the proselytizers for more spiritual accomplishments, among them the moral education-alists Hannah More and Maria Edgeworth, whose writings were first published at the end of the eighteenth century and were still enjoying new editions in the late 1820s. Propriety, virtue and piety,

The morning call, 1830. The artists of the Drummond watercolours were the children of the family. In this drawing tightly-laced ladies, concealed under layers of petticoats, silks, voluminous sleeves and hats, sit bolt upright and engage in idle chatter – a contrast to the Hardens' informality and industrious leisure.

they proclaimed, should be the goals of women, and particularly those of 'rank and fortune'; instruction for women should be to train them as 'daughters, mothers and mistresses of families'. The accomplishments of the drawing-room should serve only these ends and not become ends in themselves. The purpose of learning music was not to become celebrated in it; rather it should be regarded as 'merely forming a branch of moral discipline, by trying the temper, and exercising the patience', counselled a mother in a letter from the Drummond Album. Hannah More wrote of women: 'Their knowledge is not like the learning of men, to be reproduced in some literary composition nor *ever* in any learned profession, but is to come out in conduct.'

This morality was deeply rooted in religion and puritan principles of self-discipline, hard work and reward for virtue. 'Religion', wrote Fanny Drummond, having learned her lessons well, 'should mingle with everything, should give motive for exertions, solemnity to punishment and add pleasure to reward.' Passion (meaning temper), obstinacy, disobedience and idleness – for Maria Edgeworth 'the root of all evil in children' – were errors to be prevented when possible and to be corrected when prevention failed. A system which was powered by prayers, reinforced by punishment and occasionally encouraged by reward was usually employed. However, even Maria Edgeworth would have disapproved of the backboards, those instruments of torture which

OPPOSITE AND ABOVE *Scenes of punishment and pain, c. 1828. The small girl opposite has been severely chastized with a birch for having thrown her backboard on the floor. The boy summons a servant, possibly to take the girl to her room. Meanwhile a piano lesson continues, uninterrupted by the drama. The two chief instruments of the children's torture are portrayed again in the drawings above: on the left, another discarded backboard lies on the floor, with a birch ominously ready on the shelf above; on the right, a backboard in use: a girl stands 'uncomfortably trussed up like a turkey'.*

ABOVE *The schoolroom, 1828. Gaily striped chair-covers and matching red festoon curtains contrast with the seriousness of the children's round-the-clock instruction. Fanny Drummond recalled that slates were placed next to their beds at night with self-examining questions to be answered by morning.*

RIGHT *Easter Sunday, 1829. Moral confinement seems to have led to physical confinement also, as witnessed by the small girl dressed up and hatted in emulation of the adults. The freedom of children to wear unrestrictive clothing, fought for by Rousseau in the eighteenth century, was fast declining in Victorian England.*

LEFT *The morning toilet, 1829. Floor-length flounces and pantaloons conceal the legs of children, women and tables alike.*
ABOVE LEFT *A manservant in livery.*
ABOVE RIGHT *The housekeeper, Mrs Fitzherbert; only her white apron denotes her station, as female servants did not yet wear livery.*
RIGHT *Visiting a sick maid, 1827.*

the poor Drummond girls had to suffer.

Misses More and Edgeworth inspired a number of other writers such as Mrs Trimmer, Mrs Sherwood and Mrs Chapone, all of whom confirmed the idea that spiritual education for women was primarily a means for securing domestic happiness. In this sense it was women themselves who helped create the Victorian idea of the woman's role as one of total submission and dependency on men, and who encouraged their confinement to the home. Their didactic writings derived from the eighteenth century when the general immorality of the times provoked a number of religious zealots from John Wesley onwards to challenge a profligate Establishment. Moral reform gradually spread from these Nonconformists to all sectors of society until, during the nineteenth century, it not only permeated all the classes, but also both the established and disestablished church, helped considerably by these proselytizing women educationalists. It was the children reared according

LEFT AND ABOVE *Family games, 1828–9. A predilection for pranks and party games seems to have been common to both children and adults alike. In the game of charades on the left, the Drummond children's father kneels in mock abeyance to the young Lord Palmerston, later Prime Minister. All ages join in the rumbustious game of cock-fight shown above.*

Blind-man's buff, c.1828. A happy release from lessons.

to their principles, children like the Drummonds and even Queen Victoria herself, who were to set the tone for the century.

The instilling of lessons of morality and behaviour in middle- and upper-class children was one of the factors instrumental in their gradual removal from society. Children had once mingled freely with adults in the public life-style of the Middle Ages, but now they became more and more excluded from adult life. Both the growing concept of class, which by the eighteenth century precluded mixing outside one's own, and the strict moral code by which many parents sought to raise their children prohibited the free intercourse that children had hitherto enjoyed. They had at all costs to be protected from undesirable influences. This led to their continual sequestration and, in the home, this meant greater confinement to areas designated for their own use. As the nineteenth century marched on, architects' plans, whether to improve old houses or to build new ones, included 'the children's wing', 'the children's floor' or 'the children's quarters'. Cloistered more and more in these areas and cared for variously by nurses, governesses or tutors so 'that they might never fall into the hands of servants', as Fanny Drummond wrote, children emerged from their nether regions at regular and regulated intervals unless otherwise forbidden. A common punishment was to withdraw their after-tea visit to the drawing-room.

The Drummond children grew up in a period of transition when the exponents of liberty were being challenged by those of authority, and the children's upbringing reflected this conflict. The rumbustious party games played with their parents and relations, fishing parties with their cousins on the River Colne, and family picnics and excursions were all enjoyable relief from serious lessons and punishing backboards. The scenes the Drummond children recorded are charged with the energy of their activities and emphasize the difference between the relaxed, informal Harden household and their own carefully carved-out lives in which there was a clear division between work and play.

THE BOSANQUETS

'The Bosanquetini or select views of several mansions, villas, lodges, and principal Residences of a distinguished family ...' was how Charlotte Bosanquet inscribed an album of her drawings showing the exteriors of houses belonging to members of her family. A companion album contained some forty or fifty drawings mainly of the libraries and drawing-rooms of these houses, most of them made in the early 1840s, presumably while Charlotte was visiting her many relations. Her family was descended from a Huguenot, David Bosanquet, who with his brother Jean (who remained a bachelor), arrived in England in 1685 after the revocation of the Edict of Nantes. By the nineteenth century David's descendants were an established part of the English gentry.

Charlotte's drawings reveal a strong similarity in the arrangement and atmosphere of the rooms in the houses of her relations, irrespective of their varying degrees of prosperity or their preference for a particular style. Their homes seem to exemplify the 'lived-in' look, an aim particularly sought by one of the contributors to J.C. Loudon's influential encyclopaedia on architecture and taste published in 1833. Describing how the library and drawing-room should appear in his 'beau idéal' of an English villa, he wrote 'nothing gives a room a more dismal effect than an appearance of idleness, everything should be arranged both here [the library] and in the drawing-room, as if persons using the rooms had been employed in some way or other'. The Bosanquet rooms, each with a table in the middle on which books or writing materials are lying, seem to correspond with this advice. They also share the same informal arrangement of furniture which the writer recommended. This was a fashion observed by the traveller Louis Simond in 1811, when he visited Osterley Park near London, then the home of the Earl of Jersey, where eighteenth-century formality had been replaced with 'tables, sofas and chairs studiously dérangés about the fireplaces, and in the middle of the rooms, as if the family had just left them ...'. Over twenty years later, through his encyclopaedia, Loudon was urging his readers to arrange their homes likewise, which shows how fashions that originated in aristocratic circles slowly permeated through society.

This way of arranging rooms was perhaps encouraged by improvements in lighting and, to quote Loudon, in 'improved modes of heating used in

LEFT *The drawing-room, 78 South Audley Street,
London. 1843. Charlotte Bosanquet's drawings and
watercolours record the comfortably furnished interiors
of the homes of her numerous, upper-middle-class
relations. Her own drawing-room in South Audley
Street, furnished in the contemporary taste, contains a
large upright piano with an hourglass stool, a carpet
with a new diamond-trellis design, completely covered*
*soft furniture, upright chairs of a style popular in the
1840s, as well as the ubiquitous centred table.*
ABOVE *The drawing-room, Forscote, near Bath,
1849. A contrast to Charlotte's room is her brother
Edwin's drawing-room at Forscote. His Chinese
Chippendale chairs and Pembroke tables were of a style
considered old-fashioned in more elegant circles where
they were either relegated to the attic or sold for a song.*

ABOVE *The drawing-room, Osidge House, Southgate, Hertfordshire, 1842. Osidge was the home of another of Charlotte's brothers, Augustus Bosanquet. The large expanse of patterned carpet (a characteristic of all the Bosanquet homes) is a reminder of how extensively carpet was used in the 1830s and 1840s.*
RIGHT *The drawing-room, Cockenach, near Barkway, Hertfordshire, 1842. The furniture at Cockenach is covered in washable slip-covers. Such covers, which could completely alter the character of a room, were widely used at this time. Their expendable nature, and the fact that they were removed for important occasions, has made pictorial records of them rather scarce. The practice of using covers to protect rare needlework and other unwashable upholstery, even no doubt to hide shabbiness, and of harmonizing such covers with the carpets and curtains, was recommended by Thomas Chippendale in the 1770s and continued throughout the nineteenth century.*

The library, Hamels Park, Hertfordshire, 1842. Hamels Park (now known as Crofton Grange) was largely rebuilt between 1830 and 1840 in the Elizabethan style. Remodelling was a fate suffered by many houses at this period. The library has a 'Jacobethan' ceiling, a term coined to describe the pseudo-Elizabethan and Jacobean decoration and furniture popular at the time. This library is no scholarly copy of an Elizabethan interior but, rather, the imaginative creation of a fashionable decorator.

The drawing-room, Meesdenbury, Hertfordshire, 1843. Two of the styles popular in the 1830s and 1840s, described as 'Grecian' and 'Tudor' in Loudon's encyclopaedia, can be seen in this room. A characteristic of Tudor, or Elizabethan, was the spiral turning on the furniture; in fact this style was not Elizabethan but late Stuart in origin. The numerous pieces, arranged to fill as much space as possible, anticipate the crowded interiors of the late nineteenth century.

connection with open fires, which by raising an equal temperature in every part of the room, lessen the inducement for the company to collect round the fire'. The Hardens moved their furniture to be near the fire or the light, whereas the Bosanquets apparently used theirs *in situ*. This suggests that there was some improvement in heating, though for many people the temperature in English houses remained inadequate. Another factor which affected the arrangement of the furniture was the increasing number of upholstered couches, ottomans and easy chairs which now appeared. They came in every shape and size and were no longer designed to stand against a wall. Such pieces reflected the growing desire for comfort, which might explain why the writer in Loudon's encyclopaedia urged his readers to create an impression of industry in their rooms, as if to help mitigate any suggestion of idleness which their armchairs and sofas might imply.

The Bosanquet rooms managed to strike a happy balance between comfort and industry, all without a hint of vulgar taste – a fault frequently found with homes and one which Loudon's encyclopaedia sought to help the public avoid. Whether the Bosanquets' success in eschewing vulgarity was due to reading works like that of Loudon or due to the fact that they were a socially established, well-educated family is difficult to determine. They were certainly conscious of their social position: when Jacob Bosanquet's sister, Susannah, married James Whatman, a man in 'trade' – a paper manufacturer – Jacob was furious.

However, Jacob must have relented or the social climate changed, for Jacob's son joined Whatman's flourishing business. The desire to create the right impression led to a conformity of manners and taste amongst people of the same social standing. The similarity of the Bosanquet homes was echoed in the drawing-rooms of London houses, where, as A.E. Richardson observed: 'The comedy was that so many of these rooms were alike.'

RIGHT *The drawing-room, Hollington House, East Woodhay, Hampshire. 1843. This room contains many of the ingredients prescribed by Loudon to give 'elegance' to the drawing-room: these include a white marble fireplace, pale, rose-pink walls and apple-green curtains and upholstery (Loudon approved the combination of these two colours), a white ceiling and, lastly, a round table on which a book of prints lies open, ready to provide instructive diversion. The eclecticism of the furniture, which includes a pair of bobbin-turned chairs, demonstrates the catholicity of styles found in many upper-middle-class homes in the early Victorian period.*
OVERLEAF *The drawing-room, White Barns, Hertfordshire, 1843. The curtains provide an example of the practice of forming a continuous upper drapery to unite windows along the same wall; in this room a swag with a fringed valance has been draped over a pole.*

AN UNKNOWN HOUSE

Three watercolours of a living-room and study in an unidentified house show that simple and plain furniture could be found at a time when the excessive use of ornament was widespread. The elaborate pieces which were displayed at the Great Exhibition of 1851 had very little in common with those in this middle-class home. The upholstery on the chairs, the built-in seats (often known as Turkish corners) and the deeply-fringed curtains were in a matching floral design of a discreet scale, unlike the large sprawling naturalistic patterns which proliferated at the time and were criticized by a number of designers.

PREVIOUS PAGE *The study* ABOVE *Two views of the living-room; watercolours of an unknown house, c. 1850. The study is furnished with a variety of chairs and couches, including a Turkish corner – an arrangement for seating in the corner of a room, an adjustable chair (in front of the fire) of a design which continued to be manufactured into the 1880s, a traditional basket chair, and two typically mid-Victorian drawing-room upright chairs with cabriole legs and a variation of the balloon back.*

The walls of the living-room are divided by a dado which has been painted to simulate wood, a device which was frowned upon by the 'truth' school – John Ruskin and his followers – who condemned the imitation of one material by another. Above the dado a stone-coloured wall serves as a discreet background for prints hung in symmetrical patterns in conjunction with the furniture. The decorated running border was a device popular in the 1840s. Two bookcases of light oak, a conversation sofa – variants of which were made from the 1840s to the

mid-1850s, and a circular table, are also examples of the contemporary taste. On the piano stands a pair of moderator lamps, so named because the oil was moderated by being forced up a small central tube to the wick by means of a spring-operated piston. This was the most widely-used type of oil-lamp until the introduction of kerosene (or paraffin) at the end of the 1860s.

The upholstery and furnishings, predominantly crimson throughout the two rooms, and the black-fringed pelmets, reflect the drift away from the lighter colours favoured in the early 1840s.

A TOWN HOUSE

The room illustrated here, together with a design for a drawing-room from Henry Lawford's catalogue, shows the influence which some furniture manufacturers had on their public. Lawford was one of a number of furniture designers and manufacturers in the mid-nineteenth century who made furniture for the middle classes. His rococo-inspired room was one of the most popular of the historical styles which proliferated at that time. The rococo revival owed its origins to the furnishings and decorations designed by Benjamin and Philip Wyatt for Crockford's new clubhouse, which opened in London in 1827. Their Louis xiv furniture and decoration met with opposition from a number of architects and designers who anticipated that what had begun as a revival of the baroque would degenerate in the hands of the untutored into 'indiscriminate borrowings from the rococo trivialities of Louis xv'. These prescient criticisms voiced by the architects J.B. Papworth and C.R. Cockerell did not stem the commercial success of the style, alongside other revivals, into the 1900s. Chairs similar to Lawford's of 1855 were still being made by C.R. Light in 1881.

One aspect of rococo was that it cultivated ease and comfort, expressed in the drawing-room by *fauteuils*, sofas and commodes. In this respect it is not surprising that it should have been popular in the nineteenth century when people were engaged once more in the search for comfort. Another aspect was the richness of its decoration: the white-and-gold painted plaster, gilded mirrors, gilt chairs and ormolu-mounted furniture were all ways of displaying wealth, and were thus guaranteed popularity with those who had newly come by their fortunes. On the other hand, it is something of a paradox that a style which was in essence a celebration of light, grace and nature in all its forms should have been adopted by a people as prudish and puritanical as the middle and upper classes were, outwardly at least, in the mid-nineteenth century. Perhaps it was their mistrust of pleasure which ultimately caused the transformation of Régence and Louis xv furniture, with its delicate and sparkling curves, into pieces renowned for their dark, heavy and cumbrous forms. It was this French-derived furniture and decoration, at the time erroneously called Louis xiv Revival or sometimes simple the 'Old French' style, to which William Morris and others so strongly reacted.

The bedroom from the same town house (see p. 18)

closely resembles another design in Lawford's 1855 catalogue. In this room, however, in contrast to Lawford's design, the cabriole legs of the balloon-back chairs are discreetly hidden under drapes. These drapes, together with those on the dressing-table and padded shell-shaped chair – a convention already apparent in the Drummond bedroom on p. 40 – corresponded with the current fashion of multi-petticoated skirts hiding their wearers' legs. Inter-play between furniture and fashion was nothing new. Fashionable women at the end of the eighteenth century who reclined, like Madame Récamier, on their delicate couches were only able to do so because of their recently narrowed skirts. In 1858 *The Times*

reported the widening of the door of the private entrance to St James's Palace before the wedding of the Princess Royal; presuming it to be in deference to the prevailing fashion, it said that the door was 'now capable of admitting crinoline of any amplitude'.

ABOVE *Design for a drawing-room from Henry Lawford's furniture catalogue, 1855.*
RIGHT *Drawing-room in a town house; watercolour by Samuel Rayner, c. 1855.*
The town house drawing-room is almost a realization of the Lawford design. The Louis XV inspired furniture, designed 'en suite', stands in a rococo setting of white-and-gold arabesques.

QUEEN VICTORIA

CLAREMONT

Home for Queen Victoria until her accession had meant Kensington Palace. Her attachment to it was mainly because she had been 'born and bred there', rather than any liking for its architecture. Wren's elegant Parade Rooms, one leading into another, struck her as inconvenient and lacking in privacy. Reminiscing in 1872, she decided that 'Claremont remains as the brightest epoch in my otherwise rather melancholy childhood. . . .'

Claremont and its beautiful grounds, some fifteen miles south of London, were the work of Lancelot (Capability) Brown, and were originally designed for Lord Clive of India. The Crown bought the estate for £66,000 as a residence for Princess Charlotte and Prince Leopold on the occasion of their marriage in 1816. It was to be their own private property in all

The Queen's sitting-room at Claremont; watercolour by Joseph Nash. 1848. The pink patterned paper hung with animal portraits and landscapes, and the chintz-covered chairs, seem closer in spirit to the country houses of many of the Queen's subjects than to a palace.

respects except for the right of disposal. When Princess Charlotte died there in childbirth only one year later, Prince Leopold continued to use it as his country seat. Both his sister the Duchess of Kent and his niece Victoria were frequent visitors; when he became King of the Belgians in 1831 and no longer required the house, they had full use of it. Thus it became something of a second home to Victoria.

Of her first visit there with Prince Albert after their marriage in 1840 she wrote,

the dear place looks so nice & all the rooms upstairs, are just the same, which made me think of happy days spent here in my childhood . . . [we] dined in the old Dining room & sat afterwards in the yellow Drawing room. It seemed to me like a happy dream to be here with my husband.

Perhaps it was the happy memory of that drawing-room which later prompted her to have a yellow drawing-room in her new house at Osborne. Claremont was sufficiently small in scale to provide that aspect of a 'home' which something in her character from time to time demanded. Indeed so successful was Claremont in fulfilling its role as a home that Lady Lyttelton, her lady-in-waiting at the time, wrote that 'it requires all the pages and scarlet footmen one runs

The Queen's birthday at Claremont, 24 May 1847; watercolour by Joseph Nash. The Queen's gifts have been inventively displayed, under Prince Albert's direction, in an arrangement remarkable for the complex use of flowers and greenery.

against to prove it a palace at all'. On one occasion there her household only numbered eight at dinner, a truly homely number. The Queen wrote that it 'was the smallest party I ever remember, but very nice and snug'.

Days spent at Claremont were essentially holidays, except for a rare council meeting. The day might start, after breakfast, with the Queen giving a religious lesson to her eldest child, Princess Victoria, after which both the Queen and the Prince would question their daughter about it. That over, the hours were spent in sketching, lithography, etching, driving in the pony phaeton, long walks in which Albert taught the Queen the names of plants and flowers, playing with the young children. Albert was in his element too – there was nothing he liked more than *'Das Landleben'* (country life). After dinner, during which the Band of the Queen's Life Guards had perhaps played, the evenings were passed quietly with games such as écarté, tactics and whist, and sometimes singing and piano-playing, ending with bedtime at 11.00 p.m. For some, such domestic peacefulness was too dull: 'BORING CLAREMONT!' wrote Lady Lyttelton, softening it a little by saying she believed that the garden was the most beautiful all the year round that she had ever seen, but that scarcely made up for the 'stiff dinners, ditch water and cold bedrooms'.

BUCKINGHAM PALACE AND WINDSOR CASTLE

Neither Windsor Castle nor Buckingham Palace, Queen Victoria's principal residences, could provide the autonomy or privacy of a family home. They were not her private property, but belonged to the Crown. Like other public buildings and royal residences, they were administered by the newly reformed Office of Woods, Forests, Land Revenues, Works and Buildings, commonly known as the Office of Woods and Works or sometimes Woods and Forests. Headed by a board of three commissioners, the First Commissioner and two juniors, the Office performed to all intents and purposes the functions and role of a landlord. Thus the Queen, ironically, was its tenant and experienced all the difficulties inherent in such a relationship. The commissioners were first and foremost servants of the public rather than the sovereign, and implicit in their appointment was that 'they should be a check upon any extravagant act' – a proviso no doubt thought up by a Parliament tired of the extravagances of George IV's building activities. The practical consequences for the Queen of having such a landlord were that all structural repairs, improvements and alterations to either palace had to have the approval of the Board who would either pay for it out of money already granted by Parliament or recommend, if it thought the improvement justified, that the Treasury should request Parliament to grant further money.

As in all bureaucratic departments, its wheels turned slowly, in spite of recent reforms. Stories abounded of its inefficiency. Responsible for the exteriors of the palaces, it seldom co-ordinated with the departments responsible for the interiors, so that, for example, it was rare for both sides of the windows to be cleaned at the same time. It was dilatory in authorizing work even though urgently requested by the Lord Chamberlain on behalf of the Queen. In 1837

several alterations were required for the Queen's own private apartments: making a door between her own and her old governess's (Baroness Lehzen) adjacent room; stopping up doors which opened onto the servants' stairs; bringing a hot-water supply to her moveable bath, etc. Two years later, the new Lord Chamberlain, Lord Uxbridge, had to write to the Prime Minister, Lord Melbourne, complaining that this work requested by his predecessor was still not completed due entirely to the inertia of the Office of Woods and Works.

The trouble with Buckingham Palace was that it continually needed altering. 'It was a curiously built house . . . built with all sorts of fancies; built in fact to please George IV and Lady Conyngham [his mistress]', wrote the Queen in her Journal, quoting Lord Melbourne. William IV and Queen Adelaide never lived in it and it was not surprising that what had been designed for a bachelor would scarcely be convenient for a young woman. When the Queen married and had children its inconvenience became even more apparent. As well as the unsuitability of the accommodation for a family home, its services were quite inadequate. The drainage, ventilation and heating systems were a danger to the health of its occupants and it was only after the intervention of the Queen's physician, Sir James Clark, that the Office of Woods and Works ordered work to be done to prevent the sewer from overflowing into the kitchen in the event of heavy rain. The chimneys were also defective

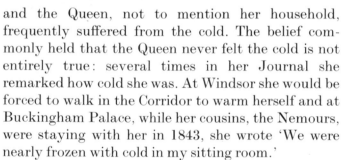

and the Queen, not to mention her household, frequently suffered from the cold. The belief commonly held that the Queen never felt the cold is not entirely true: several times in her Journal she remarked how cold she was. At Windsor she would be forced to walk in the Corridor to warm herself and at Buckingham Palace, while her cousins, the Nemours, were staying with her in 1843, she wrote 'We were nearly frozen with cold in my sitting room.'

By 1845, with four children already born and another on the way, the Queen wrote to Sir Robert Peel, then Prime Minister, of 'the total want of accommodation for our little family which is fast growing up'. Apart from the lack of nursery space, the arrangements for entertaining were quite inadequate. Eventually, on 15 August 1846, Parliament agreed to vote £20,000 towards additions to Buckingham Palace; the rest of the money needed for this work was to come from the sale of Brighton Pavilion. Even when these additions were completed Buckingham

ABOVE LEFT *Queen Victoria's sitting-room, Buckingham Palace; watercolour by J.Roberts, 1854. Portraits of the Queen's beloved Albert, her children and relations, and the curtains and chair-covers of chintz scarcely diminish the grandeur of this gilded room. On the right stands a bird-cage with a goldfish bowl on top.*
ABOVE RIGHT *The Prince Consort's dressing-room, Buckingham Palace, coloured photograph, undated.*
RIGHT *The breakfast-room, Buckingham Palace; watercolour by J.Roberts, 1850. Most of the furniture and decoration came from the Brighton Pavilion after it was sold in 1847. The painted wall and doorway decorations were from the banqueting hall and were designed by Frederick Crace, a leading decorator. The marble and ormolu mantelpiece, the work of Sir Richard Westmacott, came from the music room. The black-and-gold dining chairs, also from the Pavilion, were made in 1817, while the elaborate grate was newly designed for this room. It was used as a family room as the toys on the floor disclose.*

Palace still remained too small both as a State building and for the Queen's increasing family.

In addition to the Office of Woods and Works, the Queen had to contend with the chaotic system of administering the palaces. Responsibility for their internal arrangements was divided among three departments, headed respectively by the Lord Steward, the Lord Chamberlain and the Master of the Queen's Horse. These were secondary appointments for peers who already held high political offices, and were subject to change at each change of government. According to Baron Stockmar, Prince Albert's mentor, there were five different lord chamberlains and six different lord stewards between 1830 and

The Corridor, Windsor; watercolour by Joseph Nash, 1846. The Corridor, designed by Sir Jeffry Wyatville for George IV and completed in 1829, has all the panache associated with that flamboyant king. It was intended to be a painting and sculpture gallery, but its 550-feet length provided also a place of exercise for the Queen and a playground for her children. The Corridor glows with scarlet-covered window stools and matching curtains; Venetian paintings and English portraits; gilded candelabra and richly carved, gilt picture frames; ebony sofas, boulle wardrobes, oriental cabinets and chairs; white marble busts on yellow scagliola pedestals and dark bronzes contrasting sharply with the warm colours. 'It is the most strikingly beautiful thing you can conceive,' wrote Lady Agar-Ellis in 1829.

1841. Because of their political commitments none of them was resident in the palaces, so there was minimal supervision of the servants and orders had to be delegated to lower ranks. There was a resident Master of the Household within the Lord Steward's department, but his authority did not extend to the other departments. Since each of the three departments was responsible for various categories of servants and household duties – and since these responsibilities were neither clearly defined nor well co-ordinated – some ridiculous situations resulted. For example, the Lord Steward's department provided the fuel and laid the fires; the Lord Chamberlain's department lit them. On the other hand, the Lord Chamberlain's department provided the lamps, but the Lord Steward's department cleaned and lit them. Any request for repairs in the kitchen offices had to be made initially by the chief cook, then countersigned by the clerk of the kitchen, then signed by the Master of the Household, authorized by the Lord Chamberlain's Office and finally sent to the Clerk of Works under the Office of Woods and Works. Prince Albert reorganized this system, but it was not until 1846 that his reforms were ratified and the situation began to improve.

The Lord Chamberlain's reports and accounts give an insight into the astonishing scale of organization needed to run Windsor Castle and Buckingham Palace. Both palaces were in a continuous state of restoration, refurbishment and renewal: at any one

time there might be found in either or both of them upholsterers, decorators, paper-hangers, gilders, marble masons, pianoforte-makers, builders, picture cleaners, clockmakers, turners, scaglioliers, cabinet-makers, joiners, and so on and so forth. One of the more regrettable customs, sometimes done in the name of economy, was the altering and adapting of antique furniture, particularly old picture frames. The latter were frequently cut down to make smaller frames or converted into looking-glass frames. Old boulle and ormolu cabinets and other valuable furniture did not escape, and even a François I table was altered and made to the 'required size and regilded in best burnished gold' for the royal closet in Buckingham Palace. When extensive preparations were being made for the visit of the Emperor and Empress of France in 1855, more old furniture was

ABOVE RIGHT *The Blue Room at Windsor where the Prince Consort died; watercolour by W.Corden, 1868. When Prince Albert died on Friday, 13 December 1861, aged forty-two, the Queen was heart-broken. The Lord Chamberlain's Report for the years 1860–6 records that 'By the Queen's command, the Blue Room 202 is not to be used again.'*
ABOVE LEFT *The Prince Consort's Blue Room, Windsor; watercolour by Douglas Morrison, 1843. The Prince's study, also known as the Blue Room, was to remain unchanged likewise, the Queen told her Equerry Lord Hertford. It is furnished with his Broadwood piano, made c. 1840, a cabinet (one of four made for Carlton House) above which hangs Landseer's painting 'Sanctuary', and a French-style writing-table on which stand a pair of candles rising absurdly above their draught shades.*

altered in order to fit into the newly-decorated rooms. At other times, as the fashion for the 'Old English' style increased, the scarcity of Elizabethan furniture necessitated the making of 'old' furniture out of old pieces.

There was also a surprising amount of remaking, cleaning and purifying of bedding, as well as remaking and redyeing of curtains. Carpets too were taken up and re-laid elsewhere. One of the more curious economies seems to have been made when the Queen's closet, stairs and waiting-room at Windsor were carpeted with the old carpet which had been removed from the Corridor, while the Corridor was laid with a brand-new one.

Perhaps it is not too frivolous to say that the best clue to the scale of life at Windsor was the number of dusters which were needed: twelve hundred were ordered each year and that was only a quarter of the number which were in constant circulation.

Another disadvantage of Windsor for the Queen was the spectre of those who had lived there before her. On the first visit, after her accession on the death of William IV, she confided to her Journal: 'I cannot help feeling as though I were not the Mistress of the House and as if I was to see the poor King and Queen. There is a sadness about the whole which I must say I feel. . . .' In truth she did enjoy much of her time spent at both Windsor and Buckingham Palace, taking pride in her stewardship of great possessions and constantly referring to 'my' this and 'my' that as she looked at her vast and valuable collections of prints, miniatures, drawings and silver. Her plate, according to Lady Lyttelton, was thought to be the finest in Europe, '£65,000 worth of knives and forks and spoons, besides thirty-six dozen of plates, proportionable dishes and a perfect load of ornaments for the table (four among these, by no means the best, cost £11,000 each) all of richly gilt silver, besides the shield of Achilles in gold, and a heap of candelabra one of them weighing three hundredweight.' These were just the silver-gilt objects and did not include chased vases by Benvenuto Cellini, cups of crystal mounted in rubies, as well as countless diamonds and other gold and bejewelled items.

As John Cornforth has said, 'the need for grandeur and the desire for intimacy' were constant pulls in her life. 'My rooms', by which she meant her private apartments, was not the same as saying 'my home'. It was paradoxical that in an age which valued private property above all else the highest born in the land had to wait some years until she could say, in a letter to her Uncle Leopold in March of 1845, 'we have succeeded in purchasing *Osborne* in the Isle of Wight. . . . It sounds so snug and nice to have a place of *one's own*, quiet and retired, and free from all Woods and Forests, and other charming departments who really are the plague of one's life.' And to Lord Melbourne she could at last happily write 'we were so occupied, and so delighted with *our new* and really delightful *home*, that she [sic] hardly had time for anything'.

OSBORNE

The idea of buying a family house of their own had been in the minds of the Queen and Prince Albert since 1843. The Isle of Wight, like Claremont, another scene of the Queen's childhood, was a possible place: not only was it far away from prying eyes but there was plenty of fresh sea air for a growing family, though in the opinion of Sir James Clark, their medical advisor, it was scarcely bracing enough to do the children much good. The Queen had rejected Norris Castle where she stayed as a child because it was a castellated mansion, preferring, as her maid-of-honour, Lady Eleanor Stanley, reported, 'any cottage-looking thing to a castle for a change'. Therefore when Osborne House and Estate became available she decided to buy it. She purchased it out of her own money, thus becoming free at last from the Office of Woods and Works. It was, to her, a paradise: she wrote in her Journal that the grounds were 'delightfully private'; 'we can walk about anywhere unmolested'; 'the house ... is *so* complete and snug. The rooms are small, but very nice and the offices and stabling, very good. With some few alterations & additions for the Children it might be made an excellent home.'

Prince Albert set about furnishing the house. He bought 'simple rosewood furniture' and 'pretty chintz sofas' for the drawing-room and filled the rooms with china, ornaments and pictures. The greatest blessing, though, said the Queen, was that it was all 'our *very* own which makes it doubly nice'. However, it soon became clear that not only would altering the house be too costly but also that the house would never be capable of providing suitable accommodation. A new house was the only alternative. Prince Albert, aided by the redoubtable Thomas Cubitt, drew up sketches for a new Osborne, and the foundation stone was laid on 23 June 1845. The visits during the next fifteen

RIGHT *The Queen's sitting-room, Windsor; watercolour by Joseph Nash, undated. The early nineteenth-century gilt chairs and sofas, the elegant tables designed by Morel and Seddon for George* IV, *and the Sèvres ornaments make this room no cosier than the Queen's sitting-room at Buckingham Palace. A homely note, however, is created by the carved and gilded seventeenth-century cradle, acquired by the Queen in 1843.*

OVERLEAF RIGHT *The Queen's bedroom and dressing-room, Osborne; watercolour by J.Roberts, 1854.*

OVERLEAF LEFT *The Queen's bedroom, Balmoral; watercolour by J.Roberts. Her bedrooms at Osborne and Balmoral, even with the latter's striking tartan furnishings, disclose her preference for simplicity, perhaps in reaction to the palatial splendours of Buckingham Palace and Windsor. Both rooms contain half-tester beds, their hangings matching the covers of the sofas and chairs.*

The Reception of the Siamese Ambassadors at Windsor; watercolour by R. Landells, 1858. The Queen recorded the event in her Journal thus:

We dressed early for the strange audience of the Siamese Ambassadors, sent by the 2 Kings. All, were in full dress, I, on the throne. . . . The Ambassadors entered, 7 in number, the chief one carrying the letter in his hands. All the others, according to Siamese custom, when they reached the door, prostrated themselves, taking their helmets off, & crawling on all 4s. The letters, in a basket, were deposited on a stool, the Ambassador then also taking the same wonderful posture & reading his Address in Siamese. After presenting the letter Ld. Clarendon went up to these recumbent creatures, who look rather like Chinese, with dark skins & jet black hair, & told them I was much pleased with the presents, consisting of an Eastern crown of gold & enamel, with diamonds, emeralds & rubies, a gold collar, thickly studded with rubies, a large star, a massive ring set with different precious stones, a golden belt with rubies, a chair of state, or throne, a rare & valuable white shell, all jewelled, – an agate cup & saucer, a state palanquin, a state saddle & bridle, a number of umbrellas covered with gold embroidery. . . . In taking their leave the envoys crawled the whole way backwards out of the room, – really, it was most difficult to keep one's countenance.

months were indeed halcyon days, possession still striking the Queen as remarkable: 'It is delightful to feel we are living in our own possession.' Prince Albert closely watched over the building of his creation, supervising the laying-out and planting of the grounds. More land and adjacent properties were added to the estate. Barton Farm which lay nearby was bought to be used for the Duchess of Kent on her visits and for other visitors or members of the household.

On 14 September 1846, less than fifteen months after the foundation stone had been laid, Victoria and Albert spent their first night in their new house. Architecturally it was Prince Albert's concept of an Italian villa, with its two campaniles, niches filled with marble busts and lawns descending towards the sea. To ensure a sense of privacy the Royal Family's quarters were built as a separate pavilion attached to the main block of the house by an open colonnade. The interior of this pavilion is best described by the Queen herself.

On entering the Hall, to the right, is the Drawingroom, a simple, yet at the same time handsome room, with a bow to it, & opening into it, without a door, a handsome billiard room, with columns dividing it from the Drawingroom, but this is not yet furnished. Our Diningroom is on the other side of the Drawingroom. There are 2 spare rooms on this ground floor. A handsome staircase, much resembling the one at Claremont, brings one to our living rooms on the 1st floor, consisting of a charming bedroom (above the Diningroom), dressing room and bathroom (in one), our sitting room, a lovely room with a bow, very like the shape of mine at Buckingham Palace; opening out of that is Albert's dressing room & leading out of that his bathroom. Mounting another flight of steps one comes to the Children's quarters, nurseries, schoolrooms, governesses rooms, etc. . . . & there are also rooms for some of my maids. All is so convenient, spacious and well carried out. Mr Cubitt has done it admirably.

The rooms in relation to Buckingham Palace were surprisingly small in scale; with their picture-lined walls, plain rosewood furniture and knick-knacks, they were the realization of many a Victorian family's dream and fulfilled the Queen's own desire for the 'snug' and the 'cosy' – two of her favourite words. Osborne was furnished partly by three firms, Dowbiggin, Holland and Oetzmann, the last of which claimed to be the first store in London where the 'expanding middle classes' could have their entire house 'tastefully planned, decorated and furnished throughout'. It is not surprising that Osborne, with its royal patronage of popular taste, became an influence and inspiration for both the great mansion and the suburban villa.

For the Queen, the new house provided a perfect backdrop to idyllic days spent in much the same pursuits as at Claremont, but with the added delights of the sea and all that went with it. It had also provided a challenge for the creative energies of the Prince, which were soon to be at work again at Balmoral.

BALMORAL

Though Osborne fulfilled the Queen's desire for her own home, two disadvantages emerged: 'accessibility and a relaxing climate', as Sir James Clark had forewarned. He suggested that the dry, mountain air of Scotland would be beneficial to the Queen, who was already given to attacks of rheumatic pains. Scotland had made a favourable impression on her during her first visit in 1842; its remoteness made the idea of another home there irresistible. When the lease of the Balmoral Estate and Castle became available, the Queen and Prince took it over. Their first visit was in September 1848; they were enchanted with the little castle built in the Scottish style, the clean, mountain air, the salmon-fishing and stag-hunting for Albert and the mountain scenery for the Queen to sketch. When they returned the following year the Queen wrote, 'it seems like a dream to be here again in our dear Highland home. . . .'

Like the old house at Osborne, Balmoral Castle, in spite of additions made in 1848, was to prove too small for a Queen with a family of seven children to date and a court which moved with her. So a new Balmoral was conceived by Albert in an appropriately Scottish baronial manner, to be built out of Scottish granite. They were able to purchase the castle and all 17,400 acres of the estate. The foundation stone was laid in 1853 and the Royal Family moved in two years later. By 1856 the new house was completed and the old castle pulled down. The Queen and the Prince spent the next six autumns there. In the short span of their visits Prince Albert created a model estate, magnificently planned with specimen trees. He built new lodges to replace old bothies for his keepers, planted gardens, avenues and paths through the estate, and sited gates and fences. In all, a thousand acres were replanted.

The interior of the castle was his work as well. It was curtained, carpeted and upholstered in a blaze of tartans and thistles. More Scottish allusions appeared in figures of Highlanders made of bisque holding candelabra of ormolu-mounted hunting-horns. There were other ornaments in the same style and 'loads of curiously devised and tasteful ... articles'. The furniture was mostly of maple and other light woods, as was most of the woodwork, which carried silver locks and hinges. The Queen loved it all. Perhaps her devotion to the Prince blinded her for not all shared her enthusiasm. Sir Henry Ponsonby, her Private Secretary, wrote: 'Every private house strikes me as so comfortable after the severe dreariness of our palatial rooms here.'

Above all it was the quality of the Queen's life at Balmoral which was unique for she experienced there what it was like to be a private citizen. Nothing gave her greater pleasure than incognito expeditions into

Prince Albert's dressing-room, Altnagiuthasach, 1849. The Queen was delighted by the small-scale simplicity of her Highland bothie.

the neighbouring countryside, staying unrecognized at local inns; or her one- or two-day stops at Altnagiuthasach, high above Loch Muich, where in two shiels joined together by the Prince she lived side by side with the few servants whom they took with them. A great many of their activities involved the participation of the local Highlanders; their quiet deference towards her, as well as her own interest in their lives, created a happy relationship not unlike, as one author put it, 'the small Germanic kingdom of old fairy stories, in which a king and queen, their sovereignty always recognized, are nonetheless on a carpet-slipper basis with their subjects'.

THE MELBOURNE–COWPER–PALMERSTON CIRCLE

Three houses became inseparably linked with one another during the greater part of the nineteenth century. They were Brocket Hall, Panshanger and Broadlands, and were respectively the country seats of the Lamb, Cowper and Temple families. These families were among the cream of the Whig aristocracy, and their homes and life-styles were representative of that society. As David Cecil explained in *The Young Melbourne*, theirs was a 'normal life played out on a colossal scale'. Their huge houses stood in grounds sometimes five miles round.

The library, Panshanger, c. 1858. Portraits of ancestors hug the ceiling, forming a frieze above the bookcases in the manner of a seventeenth-century room. The two brackets on either side of the bookcases probably held oil-lamps which were taken out during the day to be trimmed and cleaned. David Copperfield would have rejoiced in the huge, floral designs on the chintzes and carpets, 'looking as if freshly gathered' as he remarked of similar arrangements on the carpet in his and Dora's home. Such realism, however, had its detractors in artistic circles.

PANSHANGER

The connection between these families and their houses was through the Hon. Emily Lamb. Born at Brocket Hall in Hertfordshire, she was the daughter of the first Viscount Melbourne and sister to Peniston, Frederick, William (the future Prime Minister), George and Harriet. In 1805 she married the fifth Earl Cowper and went to live at Panshanger which was situated conveniently close to Brocket. On Lord Cowper's death, thirty-two years later, she returned to Brocket for a short period, until her second marriage in 1839 to William Temple, then Lord Palmerston, when Broadlands in Hampshire became her home. She remained a visitor to both Panshanger and Brocket which, after all her brothers had died, she inherited.

Her marriage to Lord Cowper also brought her a house in London off Hanover Square from which she kept in close touch with the political and social events of the day. On the Ladies' Committee of Almack's, the most select and sought-after club in London, to whose balls admission was gained only by personal invitation or a restricted system of vouchers, she became a powerful force in society – a position she was to exercise to the full during her marriage to Lord

Palmerston. But until that time much of her life was spent at Panshanger where she threw herself into 'housewifely occupations', rejoicing in the newly-discovered delights of country life which had now become fashionable. 'Here I am ruralizing ...', wrote Lady Cowper, 'five children about me all well and amiable ... the Country Green as in Spring and my Garden and Conservatory beautiful. I have been driving my darling Pony Carriage ... ride every day ... and [eat] a mutton chop for breakfast. ...' She was enjoying to the utmost the upper-class ideal of the pastoral life.

Houses were expected to conform to this desire to rediscover nature. No longer required only to command fine views, they were adapted in order to bring the natural world closer by the addition of terraces extending into the landscape, French windows opening onto lawns, conservatories filled with plants, and other devices to lessen the distinction between the indoor and the outdoor worlds. It was an attitude destined not to last once the march of industrialization spoilt the view with factories and filled the air with smoke and noise. Then houses had to keep the world out, protecting those inside by screens of bushes, drawn blinds and heavy curtains. Until such time the cult for the pastoral and picturesque remained triumphant, culminating in a resurgence of romantic medievalism – a nostalgia for an illusory, ideal past. Houses sprung towers, turrets and castellations which transformed them into imaginary castles. Much of this was called improvement.

Panshanger was built according to the prevailing taste. Lord Cowper called in Humphry Repton, 'your best friend on such an occasion', as Miss Bertram told Mr Rushworth in Jane Austen's *Mansfield Park*. However, Repton's extensive plans for Panshanger were not executed and Lord Cowper built a house in 1800 for which Samuel Wyatt designed additions in 1806–7. These were completed in 1822 by William Atkinson who also Gothicized the house. The work was closely watched by Lady Cowper whose enthusiasm for these 'improvements' was boundless. In 1821, when she was supervising the laying of the terraces, she wrote, 'I cannot bear to go to London for I love this place ... our improvements are the greatest you can imagine. The terrace in the winter's sun will be heavenly.' The most spectacular alteration was the addition of a large picture gallery. Twenty years later Queen Victoria, whilst visiting Panshanger with Albert, called it a 'magnificent room'. She was equally appreciative of Panshanger's other attributes: she admired its situation, thought the house 'very pretty' and described the rooms which she and Albert were given as 'small but very cheerful and comfortable'. They consisted of a sitting-room, two dressing-rooms and a bedroom. She wrote to Lady Cowper's daughter Fanny, who was by then her lady-in-waiting, that

The sitting-room, Panshanger, c. 1858. Clutter and cosy comfort was in the vanguard of fashion.

The picture gallery, Panshanger, c. 1858.
Panshanger's fame lay in its magnificent collection of
paintings and this gallery was added to the house in
1820–1 to house some of the masterpieces, among them
Van Dyck's 'John Nassau and his Family' and
Rembrandt's 'Equestrian Portrait'. By the time this
photograph was taken the gallery had been furnished as
yet another sitting-room, an example of the breakdown
in the distinction between family and state rooms which
occurred in great houses during the nineteenth century.

they 'were quite delighted with Panshanger'.

Queen Victoria was fortunate perhaps that she visited Panshanger during the summer, for Lady Cowper's 'improvements' did not apparently extend to the heating arrangements in the house. Charles Greville, the political diarist, while staying there one January, found his room so cold that he 'could not sit in it to write'. Other guests similarly suffered, saying that they were too cold to hold a pen or that, when driven downstairs by the cold, found the drawing-room too crowded to write in. It was still a common experience for visitors to country houses to suffer from the inadequacies of the heating; some would say it still is. Southey's fictional traveller in England, Don Espriella, after being 'scorched on one side and frostbitten on the other', asked, 'Why do you not warm your rooms like the Germans . . . and diffuse the heat equally on all sides?' 'It is so dismal not to see the fire,' was the reply – a sentiment which seems to have remained throughout the century. In spite of great improvements in the technology of central heating during the nineteenth century, open fires were still being recommended as late as 1880 as the best system for heating English houses.

However much they complained, Lady Cowper's guests continued to come in their numbers and fill her house. The Hollands, at whose home in Kensington the most famous salons in London were held, would arrive in a coach-and-four, with a chaise-and-pair carrying two footmen, a page and two maids. The

Cowpers' house parties seldom consisted of less than four or five couples, most of whom would bring their own servants, though not perhaps as many as Lord and Lady Holland.

It was however for her children as well as for her husband that Lady Cowper entertained. She had five children in all; George ('Fordwich'), William, Charles ('Spencer'), Emily ('Minny') and Frances ('Fanny'). It was over the Christmas periods that she really 'exerted herself manfully or rather womanfully to make the dear children pass a merry Christmas. . . . Snapdragon and games of all sorts every night'. On one occasion Princess de Lieven, the wife of the Russian Ambassador, was a house guest; she introduced the Cowper children to the German custom of Christmas trees long before Prince Albert was to do likewise at Windsor. Each child was allotted a Christmas tree which, lit with coloured candles, was placed in a pot on a table. Around it were arranged the presents to be given to the child. The climax of the Christmas celebrations was a New Year ball which became an annual event. Lady Cowper proudly related how she lodged 'twenty-six people and children' after one of the balls. They were 'brilliant' occasions with grown-ups and children all dancing together. She had all the neighbourhood – nearly 150 people – as she told her brothers:

. . . a very handsome supper, and the house and pictures very well lighted up, and the suite of rooms really looked beautiful, for I closed the Ante-Room door, and made everybody pass thro' the billiard room which was turned into a tea and refreshment room, and the Drawing Room was used for dancing. They danced with hardly any intermission from 8 till two o'clock – Minny was out of her wits with joy, danced every dance and looked beautiful.

Between these annual festivities there were long quiet stretches for the children. The Cowper parents spent much time visiting, particularly staying in Brighton. On one occasion Lady Cowper wrote how she had been away two months from her 'little children'. In later years Fanny recalled how lonely her childhood had been. The nursery was ruled with a rod of iron, first by a Mrs Hawk and then by a Miss Tomkinson, who was so strict that Fanny gave her a cat's-eye once to propitiate her.

This was the age of religion, and the Cowper children like the Drummonds were products of the age. They were imbued with a sense of duty and moral rectitude, both largely inculcated in the nursery by governesses who considered it *their duty* to form the characters of their charges. The Cowper children and their mother became, according to Greville, 'a shining example of the religion of the fashionable world and the charity of natural benevolence, which the World has not spoiled'. They not only went regularly to church (even though they arrived half an hour late owing to Lady Cowper's incorrigible unpunctuality), but also were committed to caring in both a practical and spiritual manner for the needy, beginning with their dependants in Panshanger. Together with their mother the children visited, and gave money, medicine and comfort where necessary. They became 'furiously Protestant and anti-papal', representative of the new seriousness and commitment to religion which characterized their generation. They were unlikely to have regarded their good deeds with the same levity as their mother who had written, with some humour, ten years earlier, 'I have been doing all sorts of proper things so have laid up a store of indulgences for all the improper ones I shall do. . . .' Times had changed: the amorality which had been the mark of many of the upper classes during the closing years of the eighteenth century and the beginning of the nineteenth had given way to morality. As Lady Cowper discovered, it had become 'the fashion to be devout'.

The Cowper children grew up and married. Fordwich inherited Panshanger on his father's death in 1837 and lived there until he died in 1858. William became groom-in-waiting to the young Queen Victoria in 1837; he married Georgina Tollemache, inherited Broadlands from his stepfather and subsequently became Lord Mount-Temple. Spencer married twice; he lived at Sandringham in Norfolk until he sold the house to the Prince of Wales. Fanny became Queen Victoria's lady-in-waiting and the Queen's favourite of all the Cowpers; she married Lord Jocelyn who died of cholera in 1854. The Queen's partiality for the Cowper family elicited a certain amount of disapproval in some quarters. On one occasion in 1839 when the Dowager Lady Cowper, Fanny, Spencer, William and Minny were all dining on the same night at Buckingham Palace, Lady Lyttelton wrote that there were 'Coopers enough to mend all the butts and hogsheads in the world!'

BROADLANDS

Broadlands near Romsey in Hampshire dates from the early sixteenth century. It was transformed into an eighteenth-century house by John Brown and Henry Holland who together managed to combine in the house the qualities of grandeur and domesticity, thus providing a suitable setting for the family and public life which was to take place within. When Lady Cowper married Lord Palmerston she quite shamelessly used her home to further her husband's political career. After the illness of her brother, Lord Melbourne, in 1843, which put an end to his political life, she made Broadlands a rallying point for the Palmerston cause. 'Stay! We will have a party,' might well have been her motto. In London, her Saturday evening 'At Homes' became famous for the glittering company which assembled there.

The arrival of the railway at Romsey in 1847 made Broadlands far more accessible than hitherto, so that even when Palmerston was Prime Minister he could still manage to visit it fairly often. Family parties at that time were as much a feature of life as were political ones. Palmerston wrote how the whole of one

The drawing-room, Broadlands, c. 1858. At Broadlands, as at Panshanger, informality was sought. Edward Clifford remembered the 'home-like appearance of the [drawing-] room despite it being richly furnished'. Contributing to its homeliness is the bobbin-turned chair which contrasts awkwardly with the gilded chairs of the eighteenth century.

week was a family party and how 'Emily [was] happy with her children, grandchildren and great-grandchildren. The Shaftesburys & girls, Ashley & Harriet & their girls.' Fanny Jocelyn and her children were also frequent visitors. Diversions might be an excursion to Winchester – Fanny, the children and the governess going by omnibus and Lord Palmerston in his

Detail of Lord Palmerston's study, Broadlands,
c. 1858. The study, which was demolished in 1954,
was one of the additions to the house made by Lord
Palmerston. In this drawing he is shown working at his
desk standing – a famous characteristic of his.

barouche; or a whole morning spent in the garden taking photographs. Broadlands' guests were expected to join in the family life: hunting, shooting or, when nothing else was arranged, reading their books.

Lady Palmerston loved Broadlands as she had her former home, Panshanger. She wrote in 1839, 'I am very comfortable here. . . . This place is very beautiful. . . .' Later on she added, 'It is magnificent when we have company and when alone, it seems to be only a cottage in a beautiful garden. I dine, and breakfast, and sit, all in my own sitting room, and it's most comfortable. . . .'

There were always straw baskets with china jars standing on the sideboard to be filled with delicious leftovers from lunch which could be taken during an afternoon ride and given to some poor villager. Lord Palmerston was similarly charitable as the landlord. Personally interested in the welfare of his tenants and

RIGHT *The saloon, Brocket Hall, c. 1858. The ceiling was painted by John Mortimer and completed, after his death, by Francis Wheatley. The walls and furniture of the eighteenth century were covered in French flowered damask from the same period. As at Panshanger and Broadlands, an attempt has been made to turn the main reception room into a comfortable sitting-room, in this case by the 'puffing-up', for added comfort, of the splendid neoclassical sofas and by the addition of chesterfields and a number of occasional tables and chairs in the centre of the room.*

servants, he built model cottages for them and installed gas lighting. He was also a considerable sportsman – hunting, shooting and keeping race-horses. He believed riding very fast was 'capital exercise'; even when over seventy, the possible purchase of a horse for hacking was of sufficient interest for him to note it in his diary.

In 1865 Lord Palmerston died at Brocket and his stepson, William Cowper, inherited the estate. The serious youth, about whom Queen Victoria remarked that he 'talked very agreeably and cleverly about *poets writers Poetry* etc.', had grown into a liberal statesman committed to philanthropic work. He was intensely religious (he banned all blood sports at Broadlands), and deeply interested in artistic and literary matters. One of the recent visitors to Broadlands before Lord Palmerston died was the Cowpers' new friend, John Ruskin. Ruskin had become friendly with Georgina Cowper through their shared interest in spiritualism. The friendship was to blossom into a lengthy correspondence over many years, during which Mrs Cowper became Ruskin's confidante over his unhappy love affair with Rose la Touche.

The Cowpers threw Broadlands open to a variety of people who would never previously have crossed its threshold, so marking a new phase in the life of the house. Edward Clifford, an artist who was a frequent visitor, said that 'no house ever kept such open doors ... though the wretched were made so welcome, yet the wise and noble were still glad to find themselves there. . . . At Broadlands no distinctions of class were felt.' In 1874 the Cowper-Temples, as they were then called, held the first religious meeting at Broadlands, similar to American Methodist camp-meetings. It became an annual event known as the Broadlands Conference.

BROCKET HALL

Brocket Hall, the home of Lord Melbourne, where Lady Cowper was born, was designed by James Paine in the 1760s, a perfect example of a house built in the age of taste. Queen Victoria and Prince Albert visited Brocket after their stay at Panshanger in 1841. Lady Cowper, or rather Lady Palmerston as she had then become, wrote to her brother Frederick how she 'had made dear old Brocket so smart with red cloth and carpets, and ornaments and flowers'. In spite of this attention the Queen still thought that 'the house has a deserted look and needs furnishing and being lived in'. The architecture too she found 'unremarkable', which is not surprising as it was quite out of fashion: the Adam style or anything resembling it was much too spindly for early Victorian taste. However, what was found wanting in the place was more than made up for by the presence of her beloved Melbourne. 'I can't say how pleased I was to see Brocket, the place belonging to my good kind Ld Melbourne, and where he spent his earliest years.'

THE DUCHESS OF KENT

From the early 1840s both Frogmore House at Windsor and Clarence House in London became the residences of the Duchess of Kent, the mother of Queen Victoria. It was a significant moment in both their lives when the Duchess of Kent no longer lived under the same roof as her daughter. The Duchess had been widowed when Victoria was only a year old, and her life had centred entirely around her child. Constantly together day and night (Victoria slept in her mother's room right up to her accession, ostensibly as a safeguard against attempts on her life), the separation of their lives, which not surprisingly had become mandatory for the Queen, was to be a painful and unwelcome event for the Duchess.

At the time of her accession the Queen's relationship with her mother had been strained for a number of years, but since a lady of her rank and age could hardly live alone, her mother had to accompany her to Buckingham Palace. It was not until the Queen was about to marry that serious plans to find a separate home for the Duchess were at last able to be made. Early in 1840 Lord Ingestre's House in Belgrave Square was rented by the Queen for her mother. The Duchess recorded the event: 15 April 1840 'was a very sad and eventful day in my life . . . I went to my new home . . . the arrival was anything but pleasant. . . .' The Duchess's stay at Ingestre House, however, turned out to be brief, for shortly after her move there Princess Augusta, the last remaining daughter of George III and Queen Charlotte, who lived in both Frogmore and Clarence House, died. At the Queen's request, Clarence House was offered to her mother. The Queen was advised to acquire Frogmore for the Crown because its contiguity with Windsor Castle made it desirable on grounds of privacy. This was done and the house was offered to the Duchess as her country residence.

CLARENCE HOUSE

Clarence House was built in 1824 by John Nash for William IV, then Duke of Clarence. Part of St James's Palace where he formerly lived was pulled down to make room for the new building, which cost, according to Nash's estimate, £12,000. Nash connected Clarence House to the palace by a great corridor and gallery. When the Duke became King he continued to live at Clarence House, preferring it to Buckingham Palace. On his death Princess Augusta moved in and when she died, two years later, the

ABOVE *The large drawing-room, Clarence House.*
OPPOSITE *The Duchess of Kent's bedroom, Clarence House; watercolours by J. Roberts. 1861. Both rooms were old-fashioned by 1861, reflecting the taste of twenty years before when the Duchess first moved in.*

Queen appropriated it for the Duchess of Kent. A further £14,000 was spent renovating the house.

The Duchess took up residence in April 1841, determined not to find fault with anything she might find. However, as she admitted to herself, her 'good resolutions could stand very little mistakes'. Though she realized her 'people' had done their best, she nevertheless found much to be arranged and tired herself out in doing it. She appeared to adjust to the extent that she soon found her rooms 'very nice and comfortable', as she was shortly to find those at Frogmore.

There was a partial inventory of Clarence House taken in 1852 from which the size and distribution of her household can be discerned. On the attic floor there were eight bedrooms, some of which were occupied by female servants, others by male ones. This was rather an unusual arrangement for a period in which, as Mark Girouard said in his *Life in the English Country House*, 'infinite care was taken to see that men and women slept in different parts of the house'. The rooms were furnished with Holland roller blinds, a fixed stove and blower, a pierced fender, a planned Brussels carpet and a mahogany robe-press or wardrobe. Such equipment, in comparison to what was provided for servants in many Victorian establishments, was generous; in addition to which, each servant appears to have had his or her own room, apart from one room designated 'boys'. Although the practice of putting servants in dormitories had almost disappeared, it was not uncommon for two servants to share a room with one bed between the two of them. As late as 1876 *The Queen* newspaper was taking its upper-class readership to task for the miserable accommodation provided for servants.

On the floor below the attic slept the various ladies

who were a part of the Duchess's household. Her lady-in-waiting, Lady Augusta Bruce, had her own private sitting-room and her own maid, who slept on the same floor. Below the ladies' floor was the *piano nobile* on which were the Duchess's rooms. She had a bedroom, dressing-room and a wardrobe, which had been converted from the great gallery; there was a room for her personal maid and an ironing-room. Two drawing-rooms, one large and one small, and a writing-room completed her suite. The dining-room, library, conservatory, the room of her equerry – Sir George Couper, the pages' room, porter's room and an upper servants' hall, all occupied the ground floor.

The basement was a warren of domestic offices deemed necessary to serve an establishment of this size. Separating different activities was a growing characteristic in large Victorian houses, and in the servants' quarters the allocation of rooms for specific functions was seldom exceeded elsewhere in the house. There was the butler's room and his pantry, footmen's room, housekeeper's room, housemaids' room, still-room, larder, scullery, kitchen, pastry-kitchen, storeroom, and a separate office for Mr

The drawing-room, Frogmore House; coloured photograph, 1861. A crowded but essentially feminine corner, recalling the intimacy of a Biedermeier room. Most of the furniture is Regency, apart from some Victorian chairs. A portrait of the Queen hangs above the Duchess's treasured piano.

Seabrook, the Duchess's page, who together with Maslin, another page, were to be over thirty years in her service.

The Duchess died in 1861 at Frogmore. The members of her household were given an allowance to supply themselves with a year's mourning wear. They received varying amounts of £10, £6 and £5 according to their class. Her liveried servants wore crape on their left arms, hat cockades and epaulettes. Clarence House was looked after by a housekeeper especially appointed to take care of the furniture, which was of considerable value, until in 1866 the house once more became a royal home – that of the Duke of Edinburgh, the second son of Queen Victoria.

FROGMORE HOUSE

Frogmore House, or Great Frogmore as it was also known, is a pleasant walk from Windsor Castle. It had been given to Queen Charlotte by George III for use as her private residence. Built in the 1690s, it was a red-brick house which, at the Queen's request and expense, James Wyatt 'improved'. Work began in 1792: Wyatt added a second storey and a pair of pavilions on either side of the house, connecting them by a long, glazed colonnade or conservatory which stretched the whole length of the West Front. The red brick having been covered with stucco, the house was transformed into a mansion in the classical style. On Queen Charlotte's death it passed to her daughter, Princess Augusta, who lived there in the summer.

Queen Victoria recalled visiting her there when a child:

We lived in a very simple plain manner; breakfast was at half past eight, luncheon at half past one, dinner at seven – to which I came generally (when it was no regular large dinner party) – eating my bread and milk out of a small silver basin. Tea was only allowed as a great treat in later years.

After Princess Augusta's death the Office of Woods and Works bought the estate with the sanction of the Treasury out of the land revenues of the Crown. The Queen bought all the furniture with her own money at a cost of £5,300. The house and thirty-eight acres of land were designated for her own use, and she subsequently offered them to her mother. A further twenty acres were acquired by the Queen to make a kitchen-garden for the Castle, while the remainder, Shaw Farm, was to be let when the Crown found a suitable tenant. The Pleasure Gardens were to be the responsibility of the Lord Steward, maintenance of which was estimated at £300. The servants, cleaning, airing, buying coal and laying fires, all of which were estimated not to exceed £300 per annum, would be the responsibility of the Lord Chamberlain, while the house itself was to be maintained by the Commissioner of Woods and Works. The organization was all just as in the other palaces and probably equally inefficient; less than two years after she moved in, the Duchess was complaining of the dangerous state of the chimneys and the amount of work still to be done in her rooms upstairs.

However, on 12 October 1841, when the Duchess looked over Frogmore, she decided that she liked it better than she had previously thought: 'The House is very large and if it was mine I could arrange it as I liked. It could be made very comfortable.' By July the following year she was quite enthusiastic, for she wrote, 'I must say my rooms are very comfortable.' Her stays at Frogmore generally coincided with those of the Queen at Windsor, and there were daily visits between the two households. For the Duchess the 'happiest moment of the day' was breakfast at the Castle, or at Adelaide Cottage with the children. There were walks and drives; dinners at the Castle, with the Duchess usually sitting next to 'dear' Albert. There was the piano to play and pieces to compose as birthday gifts, for the Duchess was an accomplished musician. On Albert's birthday in 1843 the Band of the Queen's Life Guards played under his window as it always did on family birthdays, waking him up with a favourite reveille. That year they played as well the Duchess's quickmarch, especially composed for Albert.

Mornings were often spent letter-writing, an occupation which must have taken care of many hours, for even when the Duchess was living under the same roof as the Queen she communicated with her frequently by letter. There were portraits to be sat for, as the giving of one's picture was a common

The colonnade, Frogmore House, 1861. Like the
Corridor at Windsor, Wyatt's colonnade served as both
a sculpture gallery and a place of indoor exercise for the
Duchess: she could walk flanked by plaster casts of her
grandchildren and marble busts of her other relations.

practice. There were novels to read; one, with the
unexpected title of *The Story of a Flirt*, engrossed the
Duchess so much that she confessed to her Journal
that it 'occupied too much of her time'. Considering
that the Queen did not read a novel until she was
nineteen and then it was the fashionable Walter

The small library, Frogmore House, 1861. The Duchess's favourite chair is shown in this detail of the room.

Scott's *Bride of Lammermoor*, the Duchess's choice was rather surprising. Novel reading in certain circles was still considered rather *risqué*. One lady, according to her footman, always kept the Bible close beside her when reading a novel so as to make a quick exchange if anyone called. The Duchess played endless games of whist in the evening, at home or at the Castle. Her daughter's frequent confinements worried her: Victoria 'taken ill' was the way she noted a new birth in the family. Though Victoria and her family almost totally absorbed the Duchess's life, she was tactful enough not to impose herself too much. It was not uncommon for her to write that she had left them after a breakfast or a dinner so as 'not to be in the way'.

In contrast to the concern she felt for her family was her seeming lack of feeling for her servants, especially those whom she liked. One poor maid called Lisette wrote to the Duchess on 30 August 1850 of her intention to marry. The Duchess was so put out that she confessed, 'It was too much for my self control, it made me ill.' The subject was not mentioned again by either of them for almost two years, when Lisette reminded the Duchess that she had deferred her marriage for more than a year and asked 'when might it take place?' 'The subject still put me very much out', wrote the Duchess. She had been equally 'put out' when another maid, Emilia, left her to marry Maslin, her page.

The Duchess's attitude to her servants was reflected by many of her contemporaries. Having created a life-style which depended entirely on the support of servants, it was not surprising that they disliked anything which might threaten it. 'Followers' were invariably discouraged for that very reason. Gaining rights for servants was an uphill task firmly resisted, especially by the new rich who, for the first time, had the opportunity of becoming members of the servant-owning class. In 1844 a new monthly, *Belle Assemblée*, was pleading for a more humane treatment of servants. Thirty years later, *The Queen* was still championing their cause.

GEORGE SCHARF

George Scharf was an antiquarian, a scholar and an artist. Named after his father, a successful lithographer and illustrator from whom he inherited many of his talents, he became the secretary and subsequently the first director and a trustee of the newly-founded National Portrait Gallery. He exemplified that Victorian phenomenon, the 'professional' man.

The detailed drawings which he made of his home in 1868–9 are an extraordinarily revealing record of himself. His rooms – crammed with plaster casts of ancient and classical figures, engravings of Renaissance paintings, portraits of friends and family, all jostling for space on his walls and cupboards, with books bursting out of bookcases – exactly reflected his talents and enthusiams. It was the home of a busy, thoughtful and endearing bachelor. His possessions were there because they were an integral part of his life and work, and not, as so often, to form a part of an interior decorative scheme.

Scharf divided his time between his different interests just as he did the space on his walls. He gave as much time to the 'elderlies' (his affectionate name for his mother and aunt with whom he lived), happily joining them for a singsong or a game of cribbage of an evening, as he might give to working on an essay, meticulously observing the passage of the sun on his pictures, giving a dinner party, selecting paintings for the gallery or rushing out to record some ancient building before it became lost under the demolishers' axe. A hundred things engaged his attention and he found time for them all.

He had lived at 29 Great George Street, the first premises of the National Portrait Gallery, since shortly before its opening in 1859. Though a bachelor, his delight in his home life increased with his years, demonstrating that domesticity need not be a condition exclusive to marriage. In fact, by his forty-seventh birthday, he was confiding to his diary that he was finding 'a pleasure in home ... rarely felt before'. Gregarious by nature, he enjoyed as he did everything else the company of friends, and he recorded his numerous social encounters in over forty years of closely-written journals: smoking parties, conversaziones, soirées at the Royal Academy where he 'met heaps of friends and enjoyed himself very much'; breakfast parties with the diarist, Henry Crabb Robinson, and dinner parties both at home and away; visits to his old friend, Miss Bayley, at

plain white.

Dark crimson

oak.

crimson

y oak.

green

green

green

green

green

stone

oak

oak floor cloth.

reflecting
book in
mahogany

oak floor cloth.
y.

crimson

oil cloth.

Turkey patterned Carpet

G.S. 7th August 1859.
G.S. 11th August 1859.

Sunday 12th December 1869. Front room, second floor, towards the west, 29 Great George Street Westminster S.W. 4 o'clock p.m.

green carpet with yellow rose & angular devices on the centre being yellow and blue.

LEFT *The library* **ABOVE** *The study, 29 Great George Street, London. 1869. George Scharf's drawings of his rooms reveal his culture and scholarship. His crimson-covered mahogany furniture and crimson walls demonstrated precisely the sort of popular taste which* *Charles Eastlake and his friends condemned (see p. 121). However, Scharf's prolific interests and enquiring mind give his rooms a special character which overrides whatever deficiences they may reveal about his decorative sense.*

ABOVE AND RIGHT *George Scharf's bedroom, 29 Great George Street, London, 1868–9. Scharf's 'museum of his personal life' – which included casts from antiquity, engravings by old masters, and portraits of family and friends – overflowed into his bedroom. The hip-bath was bought from his servant Lee in 1864, transforming one aspect of Scharf's life: hitherto he had used the public baths at regular if somewhat infrequent intervals of about six weeks; now he could bathe in front of the fire which in winter scarcely raised the temperature of the room beyond 7°C. Few London houses had bathrooms before 1873.*

GS. July 6th 5.45 — 6.45. July 7th 1868.

Back room. second floor.

plain pale stone wall

glass

sky

maisonne

porphyry

floorcloth

carpet

gilt shell

pale stone in niche

Mogany mahogany

bronze

porphyry

plain
pale stone
colour

plain stone colours

stone

y.

hearth rug

w. crumb cloth

my Mother.

looking North

Top floor, front room.

G.S. 24th September, 1868.

Wimbledon and evenings with the 'elderlies'.

The greatest of all his pleasures seems to have been his own intimate dinner parties. Carefully noting down the guests and drawing a diagram of the seating-plan in his diaries, he has left many a record of such an evening. Six or eight guests, often all male, were invited to dine at 7 o'clock and liberally entertained with a menu, for example, of 'green pea soup – salmon – roast leg of mutton – salmi of pigeons – strawberries and cream – sherry and Curaçao'. After such an evening he would report that it had been 'very jolly', 'a successful dinner party', 'a lively evening' or that there was 'cheerful talk'. His servant Lee 'doubled' as waiter and earned an extra 2s 6d, while Mrs Lee prepared the dinner for which she was paid the princely sum of 5s a quarter for cooking and general services. Well-known figures in the artistic and literary world mingled happily at his table with the lesser-known.

House-keeping memoranda and accounts were as much a part of his life as was the acquisition of a major painting, so that it is not surprising to find, jotted between the purchase of a Reynolds portrait for the gallery at 270 guineas, such trifles as a bottle of sherry for mother at 4s or such comments as 'much Devonshire cream eaten last month' or 'dismissed Anne [a servant] for having a man secretly in bedroom'.

In 1869, nearly a year after the death of his mother, Scharf moved to rooms in 8 Ashley Place where he

OPPOSITE *Scharf's 'Dearest mother', watched over by a huge bust of Apollo, seated in her room on the top floor at 29 Great George Street, 1868.*
ABOVE *Self-portrait by George Scharf, at 8 Ashley Place, London, c. 1885.*

lived alone, attended daily by his servants. Towards the close of his life he suffered anxieties over his insufficient salary, stretched perhaps by the cost of several illnesses. Erisepelas and scarlet fever struck him until finally, at the age of seventy-five, he succumbed to dropsy and died. Even in his final months his delight in his dinner parties remained. Toothless and rather deaf, he still enjoyed 'roast pork followed by fried sole', even if it did require 'Portwine and Selzer' to relieve him afterwards. Quite restored by these measures, he downed the following day 'soup, pork, beef, ham, fowl jelly, stewed pears and lobster', remarking 'cheerful party' although, as he woefully noted, 'lobster does not go so far as crab'.

WILLIAM KENRICK

William Kenrick came from the third generation of a flourishing Nonconformist family, who were manufacturers of cast-iron hollow-ware products at West Bromwich in Birmingham. The family were prominent in local political and philanthropic enterprises particularly in the field of education. In 1862 William married Mary Chamberlain, the elder sister of the Liberal statesman Joseph Chamberlain, who himself married William's sister. Perhaps the connection with the Chamberlain family encouraged William Kenrick's increasing involvement in public life, for in 1877 he became Mayor of Birmingham. In the same year John Henry Chamberlain, a leading Birmingham architect (no relation to Kenrick's wife), completed his transformation of a mainly stuccoed Georgian house into a red-brick Gothic mansion for his client William Kenrick. Called The Grove, it was set in a small park of about twenty-six acres at Harborne, a short drive from the city of Birmingham. Chamberlain gave his client 'elegance and importance without ostentation', qualities recommended by Robert Kerr in his influential book *The Gentleman's House* published in 1864. It was an appropriate image for an established industrialist and public figure who did not wish to display any of the flashiness so often associated with the newly rich.

The main feature of The Grove's interior was the galleried hall, reminiscent, though scaled down, of the great hall in medieval and Elizabethan houses. A characteristic of many halls of the 1870s, particularly those built in the 'Old English' style, was that they were furnished and used as sitting-rooms. No doubt the Victorians, in their nostalgia for their medieval and Elizabethan ancestors, thought that they were emulating them by living in the hall, whereas in fact their ancestors would probably have retired to their private rooms. Another reason for the popularity of using halls as sitting-rooms was that they could be used at any time of the day by members of either sex; recently more and more rooms had become either male or female preserves and chance encounters in the hall with members of the opposite sex must have been eagerly sought by the younger house-party guests.

All the decoration and ornament of the hall at The Grove was designed by Chamberlain. Its style was a mixture of Gothic and Elizabethan, with a touch of Japanese. The naturalism of the painted plant forms on the decorative panels above the sofa, the blue-and-white tiles inset into the wooden panelling on the staircase wall and the display of oriental porcelain and pottery from Kenrick's collection gave just the right touch of discriminating orientalism. In the 1870s there was hardly a home claiming to be 'aesthetic' which did not have a collection of oriental china. This was a fashion begun by Rossetti with his craze for blue-and-white china in the early 1860s. The vogue for Japanese design was stimulated by the International Exhibition held in England in 1862, when Sir Rutherford Alcock, the British Consul General in Japan, exhibited his collection of oriental porcelain. Kenrick's collection included examples of English, Continental and contemporary 'art' pottery with pieces by artists such as William de Morgan.

The best-known room in The Grove is the anteroom, a small room leading into the drawing-room which was elaborately decorated by Chamberlain. The Grove was demolished in 1963, but this room has since been reconstructed in the Victoria and Albert Museum. Chamberlain was a passionate admirer of Ruskin, and in this room his decorations were 'a perfect synthesis of Ruskinian Italianate Gothic, combined with extreme naturalism, and here and there a hint of Japanese, particularly in the floral panels'. The unlikely mixture of Gothic and Japanese, or more fashionably, Jacobean and Japanese, was popular with other designers such as E. W. Godwin and E. F. C. Clarke. These designers tried to integrate the two quite different cultures but did not always meet with great success. The Grove, however, was the

The hall, The Grove, Harborne; watercolour by William Kenrick, 1877. An unusual feature are the tiles integrated into the design of the staircase wall.

home of a discriminating patron, and a realization of the principles which the pioneers in the reform of design had preached. It expressed Ruskin's plea for honesty in the use of materials and his love of painted decoration. In his words, it was 'built to be lovely'.

SAMUEL MONTAGU

Bayswater in the 1870s did not quite equal Belgravia either architecturally or socially, but it certainly emulated it. The wide streets with lofty stuccoed mansions standing in terraces or encircling gardens derived their inspiration from the Regency splendours of Belgravia conceived by Thomas Cubitt.

Lancaster Gate, the last of the great developments of Bayswater, was completed in 1865. Together with Cleveland Square it was the most expensive part of the neighbourhood, with houses whose rateable value exceeded £300 per annum. Lancaster Gate was a grandiose scheme. Large houses surrounded a gaunt Gothic church, and were flanked by terraces of houses facing Hyde Park. These had their own private carriage-ways in front, which were bounded by discreetly-planted lawns screening the houses from the road and the gaze of the passer-by. The principal rooms of the houses were on the first floor and led onto a deep balcony, from which an uninterrupted view of the park stretched. Scarcely more than a stone's throw from the fashionable centre of town and an omnibus-ride away from the City, the salubrity, convenience, prospect, privacy and imposing scale of

the development anticipated the needs of its future occupants. In a period when wealth was becoming an acceptable substitute for birth, Lancaster Gate attracted a distinctly new class of gentry. Intermingled with them was a sprinkling of the older aristocracy and the top of the professional classes. A countess, a marquis, a Queen's Counsel, a major-general, a judge and a knight lived side-by-side with merchants and bankers, who differed from each other by nationality, race, religion and background. The diversity of its inhabitants was a characteristic of Bayswater which is still discernible today.

It was to 96 Lancaster Gate that Samuel Montagu brought his young wife and family to live in 1873. Born in Liverpool, the son of a Jewish watchmaker, he went to work at the age of fourteen to supplement the family income. Before he was thirty he had, with the aid of a loan of £3,000, set up his own foreign exchange business and made a fortune. Rich enough now to marry, he chose Ellen Cohen, the daughter of a well-established Jewish family, to be his wife. They lived in elegant Cleveland Square where five children were born to them between 1866 and 1871, and where they kept a household staff of three nurses (one German), three maids and a manservant. When they moved to Lancaster Gate, into a six-storied house complete with a superimposed double order of columns, they probably increased their staff. Their predecessor in the house was a Mr Barnet, a merchant from Kentucky. He had kept a butler, a lady's maid, a cook, three housemaids, three nurses and a thirteen-year-old page.

Their move coincided with a new and growing cult amongst many families like themselves – the pursuit of beauty. In the 1830s and 1840s a few men such as Henry Cole, the first director of the South Kensington Museum (now the Victoria and Albert), and the painter Richard Redgrave tried to improve public taste. Redgrave, who became Superintendent of Art in the Government School of Design, launched *The Journal of Design and Manufacture* in an attempt to 'establish sound principles of ornamental art'. Their work was continued by a new generation who thought that much of the ugliness of their times was due to excessive concentration on moral self-development and material gain at the expense of culture and learning. Matthew Arnold in *Culture and Anarchy* (1869) criticized the middle and upper classes for their philistinism and barbarian qualities. Such men introduced a new ethic into the public sensibility, the ethic of aestheticism. The temple of this new religion in a family-dominated society was of course the home; and a financially-established class was ready to invest its money and dedicate its leisure to the new cause. It erupted in a 'rage for house decoration', in

An interior design by E.F.C.Clarke, 1885. The designer has tried to synthesize Elizabethan and Japanese styles: 'Japanobethan' might describe the result.

collecting works of art, being 'artistic', buying 'art' furniture and in a *A Plea for Art in the House*, the title of one of the many books on the subject. Whether taste really improved was a matter of opinion. Mark Pattinson, the Rector of Lincoln College, thought that in spite of all the talk about art, and judging by his friends' houses and upholsterers' shops, there was not much improvement.

Mrs Montagu's bizarre Japanese boudoir was in the newest and most fashionable style of this

Anglo-Japanese designs by S. Godwin

aestheticism. The taste for Japanese decoration developed partly as a reaction to the curves and bulges of over-upholstered, French-derived furniture. The exposed woodwork, straight lines and principles of construction in Japanese decoration appealed particularly to the architect E. W. Godwin. Since Japanese rooms had little furniture he invented a number of pieces which he called 'Anglo-Japanese'. These were a real attempt to follow Japanese principles of design, in contrast to the mere pastiches with which the market was soon to be flooded and which bore little resemblance to anything Japanese. 'Japonaisme' or 'japonaiserie' was, like chinoiserie, the 'European idea of what oriental things were like or ought to be like'. Mrs Montagu's boudoir was a decorator's fantasy in the style, and had little in

common with Godwin's principles. It exemplified the *Saturday Review*'s comment that 'if you make any pretension to entertaining in society, and desire to have some outlet for your taste, you could hardly help putting yourself in the hands of a fashionable upholsterer'.

At the same time as Mrs Montagu was 'doing up' her boudoir, Mr Montagu was making an outstanding collection of English silver and fine paintings, which included works by Turner, Constable and Ruysdael. He was typical of many collectors who, having made their money, responded to the ethos of the day and became cultured. A number of these collections were to enrich the national heritage through bequests to museums and galleries.

ABOVE LEFT *Anglo-Japanese designs by E.W.Godwin.*

RIGHT *Boudoir of an English lady; watercolour by Nicholas Chevalier, c. 1875. Godwin's furniture, with its lightness and domestic scale, seems to catch the spirit of Japanese design. Both qualities were welcomed as a change from the massiveness of much so-called 'art' furniture – often more appropriate to the convent refectory than to the home. Very different, however, is Mrs Montagu's pseudo-Japanese, or rather oriental, extravaganza in which she is pictured with her two daughters. Here the pursuit of beauty has led to a riot of colours, decorations and objects, in contrast to the reticence of the style from which the décor was derived.*

'THE CLIQUE'

St John's Wood, London, enjoyed a unique reputation from the beginning of the nineteenth century when small villas, hidden by high-walled gardens, were first built there. The 'rus in urbe' seclusion and privacy of these houses attracted all those who wanted a retreat, particularly 'authors, artists, bohemians, demi-mondaines'; among them was George Eliot who with her friend George Lewes moved to The Priory in St John's Wood in 1863. Also living in the area at this time was a group of painters who called themselves 'The Clique'. The original seven members, who included George A. Storey ARA, Stacy Marks and George D. Leslie, had been pupils together at Leigh's Academy of Drawing. Later they were joined by Val Prinsep and George Du Maurier. They held group exhibitions at the Dudley Gallery between 1864 and 1882 and often passed their evenings sketching in one another's houses until, in the early 1880s, the group began to disperse.

A dining-room in St John's Wood; watercolour by G.A.Storey, c. 1880. Green walls were popular throughout the century.

This watercolour by George A. Storey is thought to be of the dining-room in his house in St John's Wood. Apart from the table in the right foreground, which is eighteenth- or early nineteenth-century, the furniture including the horsehair-stuffed chairs appears to date from the 1830s and early 1840s. It is a refreshingly cheerful room, having none of the so-called 'congenial gloom' of the average nineteenth-century dining-room – the consequence of considering the dinner more important than the guests. Dark, heavy walls were thought 'to act as a powerful foil to the white draped table and its superimposed delicacies'. The light walls and the large French windows with white curtains make the room unusually bright. The light colours were also unusual in that dark ones were considered more suitable for a room lit by gas, which despite the improvements made by William Sugg in the late 1850s and the invention in 1870 of the counterweighted, water-slide adjustable gasolier (shown in this picture), still produced extremely dirty fumes. Not until the invention and development of the incandescent gas mantle in the 1890s was gas lighting considered reliable, by which time it had to compete with electric lighting.

THE PRINCE OF WALES

Apart from the residences occupied by Queen Victoria there were a number of others in which lived royal dependants and loyal retainers. These were 'grace and favour' dwellings under the custodianship of the Office of Woods, which must at times have made it seem, in the Office's diligence to protect the public purse, a doubtful privilege. When the Queen gave Lady Augusta Stanley (née Bruce) a 'grace and favour' apartment in St James's Palace on the death of the Duchess of Kent, the Office of Works (which since 1850 was no longer amalgamated with the Office of Woods and Forests) and the Lord Chamberlain's Office nearly drove her to despair. 'If you can imagine how difficult it is to get them to do anything,' she told her sister, 'I am not to have even the articles of furniture that were in it.' However the Queen must have intervened on her behalf, for there is

Princess Alexandra's boudoir, Marlborough House, c. 1890. At first sight the interior of this room looks like an extreme example of royal clutter run riot; in fact such crowded assemblages of small knick-knacks and photographs were usually highly organized, as was the 'set-piece' of larger objects in the entrance hall (overleaf).

a note in the Lord Chamberlain's report to the effect that the Queen had consented to her using some of the furniture already there.

The Prince of Wales experienced similar problems at Marlborough House. Having been given the house when he was eighteen as his London residence, he found that it involved him in continual trouble and expense. Since it was neither a palace nor a royal lodge it did not come under the custodianship of the Office of Works. This meant that expenses connected with its upkeep had to be met by special votes of money from Parliament; otherwise the Prince had to pay from his own pocket. Unfortunately Marlborough House turned out to be large enough neither for his life-style nor for his increasing family of children. In 1877, out of eighty-eight servants – twenty-nine female and fifty-nine male – seventeen had nowhere to sleep in the house, and servants of any visitors who came to stay had to be boarded out. The seventeen without sleeping accommodation were a page, a piper, a cook, a cook's apprentice, a valet, the Prince of Wales's brusher, a cellarman, two under-butlers, two pantry assistants, an usher of the hall, two lampmen and three coal porters. Even this small sample of the staff shows the variety of servants

employed to support the Prince's family. While he lived at Marlborough House his staff, both indoor and out, increased to 120.

The basement of Marlborough House was always blocked with boxes and cases of glass and china, as well as empty boxes, and when a ball was given – a not infrequent event for the sociable Prince – the entire furniture from the drawing-rooms, dining-rooms and other rooms had to be taken to the upholsterer's for want of storage space. The only room for stowing away objects had had to be turned into a drying closet, all the linen for the house having originally been dried in front of a small fire which was both

ABOVE LEFT *The entrance hall* ABOVE *The drawing-room, Marlborough House, c. 1890. Marlborough House was the social centre of London, and its opulent, crowded interior represented the taste of high society. The extraordinary 'arrangement' of unrelated objects, together with the richness of the furniture and decorations, was exactly what the avant-garde were reacting against. The French-style drawing-room was decorated in white and gold and upholstered in crimson silk, with silk draperies and cushions; added to this were oriental screens, two Broadwood pianos, statuettes, kentia palms and a host of smaller objects and trinkets.*

inconvenient and dangerous. As a result, not only the plate-room but also passages and every available corner of the house were filled with furnishings.

In addition to these disadvantages the defective plumbing and contaminated water-supply led to typhoid fever sweeping through the household in 1876. Christopher Wren's magnificent frescoed rooms, built in 1709 for the Duke of Marlborough, gave no hint of the rat-infested sewers on which they stood. When the Prince's children contracted typhoid Dr Seaton, the chief government medical officer, laid the blame on the sewers and the overcrowded conditions. Sir Dighton Probyn, Controller of the Prince's household, wrote to the First Commissioner of Works telling him that the Prince, since his occupancy in 1862, had spent £50,000 out of his own purse on new works and repairs, exclusive of decorating, and that he hoped that the 'First Commissioner will see fit to ask the Government to bear the expense of this new unavoidable outlay which must now be incurred to render the house safe for the Royal Family to live in'. £50,000 was the Prince's annual income from the Duchy of Cornwall, but the fact that he also had capital of £600,000 may have accounted for the government's reluctance to contribute more to the expenses of Marlborough House. Nevertheless on this occasion they agreed, and £1,000 to £1,500 was authorized for repairing the defective drains: 'Mr Rat must now find new lodgings.'

After Marlborough House's inadequacies as a residence for the heir apparent were shown up by illness, the anomaly of all the house's expenses falling on the Prince of Wales instead of on the Office of Works as in other royal houses was at last recognized. From 1878 onwards the Office of Works accepted responsibility for Marlborough House, though not of its furniture and fittings. Though this relieved the Prince of certain expenses, it did not render the house satisfactory, and six years later he was again finding the house too small. There was still no store-room. The Prince wanted to build one next to the stables to house valuable furniture and portmanteaux, and to incorporate in it a carpenter's workshop. Permission was refused in 1885 but reluctantly granted the following year after it was pointed out that there was a fire risk in the existing carpenter's workshop. It was so dark there that the room had to be lit by gas and, since it was always filled with furniture and in-flammable litter used in packing, it was particularly vulnerable to fire. The Prince also complained that the three princesses still occupied the same small room in which they had slept when they were little children. This meant that when the eldest, Princess Louise, went to a party she had to dress in her maid's little bedroom in which another maid also slept. The passage to the princesses' room was blocked by boxes and wardrobes like the rest of the private quarters of the house. The cellar too was inadequate, so hot and overcrowded that on one occasion £1,500 worth of

*The Prince of Wales's study, Marlborough House,
c. 1890.*

champagne was lost: due either to heat or damp the
wine was badly ullaged.

Meanwhile life upstairs flourished in a whirl of
social activity. The Prince's day began quietly with
tea and a walk in the park, followed by breakfast of
eggs, toast and more tea at 9.00 a.m. He took the meal
alone in his sitting-room since his wife did not leave
her room until 11.00 a.m. After breakfast the Prince
worked with his Private Secretary for an hour, and
then spent half an hour with Sir Dighton Probyn with
whom he could communicate by a call-pipe system
between their rooms. At 11.00 a.m. the Prince gave
interviews in his ante-room, and around noon he
visited his stables where he kept sixty horses.
Luncheon, served at 2.30 p.m., was 'open house' for
his relations. But it was in the afternoon that his
social life really began. After their marriage in 1863
the Prince and his wife, Princess Alexandra, had
plunged into a season such as London had never
known, setting the tenor of their London life: ball
followed ball; Derby Day dinners were held in the
magnificent fifty-feet-long State dining-room; tea
was served in the garden at 5.00 p.m., 'sans cérémonie',
in brightly striped tents in which cushioned garden
seats were placed on oriental rugs; small dinners were
held *à la Russe*. Dinners *à la Russe* were an innovation
in the 1860s, but having been made fashionable by the
Prince they remained the custom for formal dinners
thereafter. The term simply meant that all the dishes
of food were placed on a side-table from where the
servants handed them round for each guest to help
himself. Hitherto the serving dishes had been placed
on the central table and the meats carved there, the
guests helping themselves and each other.

The Prince's favourite entertainment was to invite
a few friends to a 'baccy', as he called a late-night
supper followed by whist or baccarat played into the
small hours. Everything was designed to fill his
underworked hours. Those who visited him regularly
earned the doubtful honour of being known as the
'Marlborough House Set'. His extravagant social life
was aped by those who could afford to, sharpening the
contrast between 'upstairs' and 'downstairs'.

GEORGE HYDE WOLLASTON

College Road, alongside Clifton College, was in a comfortable residential part of Bristol near The Downs, a large area of grass and trees bordering the Avon Gorge. Its houses were mainly Italianate villas, three stories high, built in pairs between 1870 and 1881. George Hyde Wollaston, a housemaster at Clifton College and one of its outstanding figures, lived at 24 College Road with his wife and children. He and his wife both came from gifted families; it was said that no family name figured more in the annals of The Royal Society than that of Wollaston. His wife, the daughter of Thomas Richmond, the miniaturist, and niece of George Richmond, the portrait painter, was herself very talented.

The Wollastons' home was not an expression of any 'set fashion' which, as Robert Edis said in his book *Decoration and Furniture of Town Houses* (1881), went under 'the clap-trap denomination of high-art' and tended to make 'show-places' instead of homes. Rather the Wollastons seem to have created an atmosphere of comfort and homeliness. They achieved this by the informal and asymmetrical arrangement of comfortable furniture, combined with a variety of objects reflecting their wide interests.

The dining-room, 24 College Road, Bristol, 1893. Both here and in the drawing-room (overleaf) the display of china is reminiscent of the aesthetic interiors of the 1870s when 'chinamania' was at its height.

The drawing-room, 24 College Road, Bristol, 1893.

An interesting feature of their home is the number of plants which they had. These were increasingly used to decorate rooms towards the end of the century and were a cheap and effective way to get a 'lived-in' look, a greatly desired quality. They also provided for the increasing numbers of urban dwellers a link with the country. However, the impurities in gas lighting, installed in many houses by the 1880s, restricted the varieties that would flourish, which accounted for the ubiquity of the nearly indestructible aspidistra. 'Wardian' cases – glass containers similar to miniature greenhouses – were also popular for that reason. 'Domestic floriculture' became a thriving pursuit.

EDWARD BURNE-JONES

ike their two good friends William Morris and Dante Gabriel Rossetti, Edward Burne-Jones (1833–98) and his wife Georgiana chose to live in eighteenth-century houses. Their preference not only signalled their dislike of stucco – Morris was to wish that London would be 'emancipated from stucco' – but also their sympathy with those architects who were looking for a more homely, domestic style of architecture which would replace ecclesiastical and commercial Gothic and palatial stucco. These architects developed by the 1870s the so-called 'Queen Anne' style – which was partly derived from early eighteenth-century Queen Anne architecture – as an alternative.

In 1868 the Burne-Joneses moved to The Grange in North End Road, Fulham. The house had been built in 1714, one of the first pairs of semi-detached houses in the country (the houses were subsequently connected internally) and had been lived in by the novelist Samuel Richardson. Fulham in the 1860s was still quite rural and the house stood in 'a beautiful garden of about three quarters of an acre, with a fine old Mulberry tree on its lawn, peaches against the walls and apple trees enough to justify us calling part of it an orchard,' wrote Lady Burne-Jones.

The Grange was furnished in 'The Firm's' taste, which refers to the firm of Morris, Marshall, Faulkner and Company, of which Rossetti, Philip Webb, Ford Madox Brown and Burne-Jones himself were partners at the time. Although many of the furnishings and decorations were made and supplied by The Firm, the house's uncrowded interiors had a simplicity much closer to what Morris preached than to the 'total schemes' which The Firm actually designed. The furniture, wallpapers and textiles in The Grange reflect the various phases in the development of The Firm's taste. Most of the furniture dates from Morris's and Burne-Jones's early predilection for painted furniture of Gothic form, and for plain, stout, simply-constructed pieces. There were also some slightly later 'country-type' chairs derived from traditional styles, and pseudo-Georgian furniture which represented the final phase of The Firm and was 'as good in its finish as Sheraton and Chippendale' which it sought to emulate.

The walls were hung with Morris-designed papers, ranging from his early, almost naturalistic 'fruit' designs, to some of his later, more formal designs. There were embroidered *portières*, Burne-Jones's

ABOVE LEFT *The hall* ABOVE *The first-floor sitting-room, The Grange, Fulham, c. 1898. Both rooms are decorated with Morris's pomegranate-design wallpaper, while the stairs have a Morris carpet protected by a drugget. Lady Burne-Jones's sitting-room on the first floor contains a piano decorated by Burne-Jones in 1861, a circular table by Philip Webb and two rush-seated chairs by Ford Madox Brown.*

decorated stained-glass windows, Morris chintzes and carpets (the novelist Angela Thirkell, Burne-Jones's granddaughter, recalls that she never saw the carpet without a drugget on it), green-stained or white-painted woodwork, and bare boards with oriental rugs. Everything reflected The Firm's principle of harmony and 'good and honest construction'.

To these examples of The Firm's taste, Burne-Jones added his own private possessions. There were the Dürer engravings given to him by Ruskin in 1865, reproductions of classical and Renaissance sculptures and a wide range of books which included the novels of Scott, Dickens and Thackeray, ancient and medieval histories, myths and legends and works on astronomy. These possessions and books provided the sources and marked the changes and development in the iconography of his work, the most notable of which was from an almost exclusive medievalism to an appreciation of the later Renaissance artists such as Michelangelo and Signorelli.

The Firm's taste was formed through Morris's reaction to the machine-made, commercially-produced furniture and furnishings of the day. He condemned both the system which produced them and the resulting aesthetic. He sought to revive the handicrafts of a pre-industrial age, turning to medieval and traditional sources for inspiration. Lady Mount-Temple, whose husband William (see p. 84) commissioned The Firm to decorate some rooms in St

James's Palace, gives a specific account of the kind of taste condemned by The Firm in the 1860s.

You remember our dear little house in Curzon Street; when we furnished it, nothing would please me but watered paper on the walls, garlands of roses tied with blue bows! glazed chintzes with bunches of roses, so natural they looked, I thought, as if they had just been gathered (between you and me, I still think it was very pretty), and most lovely ornaments we had in perfect harmony, gilt pelicans or swans as candlesticks, Minton's imitation of Sèvres, and gilt bows everywhere. One day Mr Rossetti was dining alone with us, and instead of admiring my room and decorations, as I expected, he evidently could hardly sit at ease with them. I began then to ask him if it were possible to suggest improvements! 'Well,' he said, frankly, 'I should begin by burning everything you have got!' I think I may be pleased with our humility, that after this insult, when our staircase needed renovation, we asked his firm to do it up for us! A Morris paper was hung on the walls, and a lovely little bit of glass by Burne-Jones filled the staircase window.

Now our taste was attacked on the other side, and all our candid relations and friends intimated that they thought we had made our pretty little house hideous! Somehow, we got to like it more and more, and now I think nearly all people confess that they owe a deep debt to the Morris & Co firm, for having saved them from trampling roses under foot, and sitting on shepherdesses, or birds and butterflies, from vulgar ornaments and other atrocities in taste, and for

having made their homes homely and beautiful.

After exhibiting in the International Exhibition of 1862, The Firm was applauded by a young architect called Charles Eastlake for 'attempting to form a new school of art furniture'. Eastlake was to become one of the most influential writers on 'house furnishing' through his articles in the *Cornhill Magazine*, *The Queen* and subsequently through a book called *Hints on Household Taste*, published in 1868 and reprinted in several editions in both England and America. The fashion for his own medieval-style furniture was well-known enough in America to be described as the 'Eastlake Style'. An article in the American periodical, *The Art Amateur*, in 1879 referred to him as the 'pioneer of the great movement of art in the household and reformer in furnishing our homes'. Like Morris and Ruskin before him, Eastlake was against the division of labour which prevented workers being involved in the design of an article. Therefore he was against mass-produced furniture, together with shams of all kinds and 'French-shaped' furniture in particular. He recommended a return to honest construction and honest use of materials. Less popular in England than America as a designer, he was nevertheless one of the first to disseminate the ideas which he shared with men like Morris and other reformers in design, and he tried to instil a more discriminating taste into the middle-class consciousness. It was probably the success of his book which led to a spate of books on interior decoration from the 1870s onwards, most of which, to quote from a review of one of them which appeared in *The Architect* magazine, 'scarcely deserve serious criticism'. His term 'art' furniture was taken up by all those who wanted to distinguish themselves by getting away from the general run of manufactured furniture. It also signalled the return of an increasing number of architects to designing furniture instead of leaving it to the foreman of the factory. E. W. Godwin, William Burges, John Seddon, Bruce Talbert, Frank Davis and Philip Webb were among the architects designing furniture at that date both for self-styled art manufacturers like William Watt and commercial firms such as Shoolbred & Co.

One of the characteristics of 'art' furniture was that it eschewed upholstered comfort. Ruskin was one of the first to complain that 'John Bull's comfort perpetually interferes with his good taste'. Burne-Jones, remembering John Henry Newman, whose Tractarianism influenced him greatly in his youth, said 'that in an age of sofas and cushions he had taught me to be indifferent to comfort'. Similarly indifferent, Morris is alleged to have said, 'If you want comfort, go to bed.' However in Burne-Jones's homes one was unlikely to find comfort in the beds for, according to Angela Thirkell, the beds in the Burne-Jones's country house in Rottingdean were as uncomfortable as their sofas. Remembering her grandparents' two houses, she wrote that:

the only comfortable furniture [they] ever possessed was their drawing-room sofa in London, a perfectly ordinary large sofa with good springs, only disguised by Morris chintzes. The sofas at Rottingdean were simple long low tables with a little balustrade round two, sometimes three sides, made of plain oak or some inferior wood painted white.

To these were added 'rigidly hard squabs covered with chintz of blue linen . . . a small bolster apparently made of concrete and two or three unyielding cushions. . . .' The sofas against the wall in the drawing-room at The Grange suggest the same uncompromising lack of comfort. Nevertheless such indifference to comfort was catching, as was Burne-Jones's representation of beauty in his paintings. Inevitably he created an image for aesthetically-conscious women in the late 1870s: like his heroines they would perch, in flowing dresses, on The Firm's hard little black Sussex chairs in Morris-papered drawing-rooms. Having helped to make art fashionable, Burne-Jones was soon wishing that he had not. Like a number of his fellow artists in the 1880s and 90s he opened his studio on Sunday afternoons for the amusement of fashionable London. On Mondays, after the invasion, he felt quite unfit for work. 'I wish London would leave London,' he remarked with his characteristically wry humour.

Burne-Jones's personality has been vividly captured in notes made by T. M. Rooke, his studio assistant for twenty-five years. Rooke recorded conversations with his master and his notes provide some rare insights into domestic life with the Burne-Joneses. Burne-Jones was constantly making the commonplace enchanting. Hating ever to be solemn for long, he hid his latent Celtic melancholy together with his troubles under a cover of childish pranks and artless banter. Rooke tells how Burne-Jones used to tease his wife, to their mutual delight, by paying her surprise visits in the morning immediately after having announced through the speaking-tube connecting their rooms that he would be sleeping late that day. This anecdote suggests that Burne-Jones's relationship with his wife remained affectionate, despite his recurring passion for women such as Mary Zambaco and Frances Graham.

His relationship with servants, especially with Annie, their parlour-maid, who remained with Lady Burne-Jones until her death, was one of paternal concern and vague wonder. He was aware of and admired the stoic qualities of servants, and their acceptance of the rigours of a life so much harsher than his own, but he did not actually want to change anything. Unlike Morris he was not involved in socialism and did not challenge the accepted order. Yet he was sensitive enough to be upset when Annie was scolded for staying out late, telling Rooke 'I can't bear servants to be sad. They're so dignified in their grief, they go about their work so quietly and nicely and say nothing about it all the time. . . .' He was also

The dining-room, The Grange, Fulham; watercolour by T.M.Rooke. 1898. The table was designed by Philip Webb in 1860, the sideboard painted by Burne-Jones, who also designed the stained-glass windows.

grateful to Annie for her inexhaustible usefulness, which included finding mislaid drawings or books, revealing it in his typical badinage: 'If I lose my honour she picks it up and brings it to me daintily wrapped up in a piece of silver paper.'

Meal-times often prompted this vein of humour and again it was usually Annie to whom it was directed. When she offered him some blackcurrant pie, he said 'Annie do you wish to offer me a stomachache on a dish . . . ?' If she forgot to offer him a second helping he reproached her for neglecting him: 'Annie,' he would say, 'I had to help myself to some more fish – you neglect me, you don't give me nearly enough of your company.' Sometimes his wife teased him along; knowing his dislike of carrots she told Annie not to give him any, saying to him, 'Relations are strained between you & carrots, aren't they Ned dear?' He replied, 'Carrots and I are not on speaking terms. When I see a carrot in the street I walk on the other side. Potatoes and I are on speaking terms merely, there's no friendship between us.

His was a humour which made him adored by children, and in his later life he found great encouragement in his young granddaughter. 'Why', he once asked her, 'was shepherd's pie so-called?' and did she not think the following a pretty verse?:

       'The shepherd's pie's his only jy?

       Pie I'll deny, and steak I'll take.'

Behind the teasing there was perhaps some criticism of the food itself for Burne-Jones had a horror of fatness. His numerous drawings of fat or 'prominent' women, as he called them, though disguised as jokes nevertheless represented real fears. He hated fatty meat and maybe he suspected that the food served up at lunch was what made men fat.

The Burne-Jones's two children, Philip and Margaret, like the Morris children, Mary and Jane Alice, were steeped in their parents' values, not least in the myths and legends of the Middle Ages. Morris was even more of a medievalist than Burne-Jones, dressing his wife as Guinevere or La Belle Iseult and creating a medieval garden like those in illuminated manuscripts for her to walk in. The children, with Philip and Margaret Burne-Jones, played games about knights and honour and formed their own secret society. Jane Alice, or Jenny as she was called, kept the records of their meetings which, with their formal rituals, would have done honour to any brotherhood of knights. Rules were written in a law book. In a swearing-in ceremony each member in turn sat on a throne and promised on oath to obey the laws, after which, with blackened faces and 'a fury fountain blazing in honour of each member', their ranks were assigned. There was a secret alphabet which had to be continually revised as Burne-Jones kept deciphering it. They had arms, a standard-bearer and burnt incense throughout the meetings. Transgressions were punished by loss of rank, imprisonment or a number of lashes. Jenny Morris calmly related how, having left the room without asking permission, she

EDWARD BURNE-JONES

had to suffer fifty lashes. Tasks attempted by the society included placing a step-ladder under the trap-door to the garret, raising it and entering, unlocking a door onto the roof and returning, without, one assumes, being discovered. Like their parents, the children had their dream of a world where heroes, fairy queens and shining knights in armour reigned.

Lady Burne-Jones said that they never did what is called 'entertaining' but, 'as far as we could, kept open house in a simple enough way'. For over twenty years William Morris would come for breakfast on Sunday mornings and stay for lunch. Friends were numerous and reflected, as did everything in the home, those aspects of life which were important to them. Artists, writers, musicians, actors and patrons visited them. The best testimony to the kind of hospitality which radiated from the household came perhaps from Lady Burne-Jones's nephew, Rudyard Kipling, who often stayed at The Grange when he was a child. After Burne-Jones died, Kipling hung the iron doorbell from The Grange outside his own house in the hope that the happiness which he had felt on ringing it would be passed on to other children. For him The Grange had been a paradise where the world of children and grown-ups mingled amidst paint and pictures, fun and games and music and poetry. To Burne-Jones himself his home became more import-ant in his later years. He said he hated leaving his 'interesting books' for a fashionable dinner party whose lavishness was bound to offend his fastidious

nature. He told Rooke that evenings spent at home with 'Phil, Margaret and the Missus were the nicest and holiest of them all'.

The centre of The Grange was the studio, either the house studio on the first floor or the later-built garden studio. Burne-Jones never went into one studio whilst working on a picture in the other: 'I can't live in two studios at once. . . .', he said. His studio was never a show-place like Alma-Tadema's or Lord Leighton's, but 'a maze of slightly poised objects with but narrow paths between them'. Burne-Jones took 'a positive pleasure in perching cups and other fragilities on the edges of shelves and corners of studio boxes when he used to make them sit as a cat does looking down on the dangerous depths below'. It was, Rooke said, 'a way of asserting his masterhood in his own work-room'. The day began in the studio with instructions on the day's work, after which Burne-Jones would accompany his work with 'talk of the widest subjects – always glittering with vivacity'.

One of the subjects which engaged his ever-inquiring mind was music, which also played an important part in his domestic life. Pianos in particular aroused his interest: 'I have been wanting for years to reform pianos, since they are as it were the very altar of homes, and a second hearth to people.' Their ugliness dismayed him and consistent as ever (to paraphrase Morris) in having nothing in his home which was not both useful and beautiful, he decorated first his little upright and, when it had to be replaced,

ABOVE *The drawing-room, The Grange, Fulham;
watercolour by T.M.Rooke, c. 1898. A Cairene table,
Arab oil-lamp and Persian rugs blend with the Morris
wallpaper, Benson's bookcase and Dürer engravings.*
OPPOSITE *Another view of the drawing-room.*

designed with the help of W. A. S. Benson another
piano which Broadwood built. Benson, a great
admirer of Morris, was a designer and maker of
furniture and articles for domestic use who worked
mainly in metal. The piano was made of oak, stained
green, with the black keys transformed to matching
green. The bulging legs of ordinary Broadwood pianos
were straightened out and all other protuberances
commonly called ornament were dispensed with.
Burne-Jones decorated a number of other pianos,
including a famous one for his patron, William
Graham, which was one of his greatest decorative
works. He also made a clavichord for his daughter.
The ability to play the piano and sing was expected
from cultivated women in the nineteenth century and
Lady Burne-Jones was no exception. To these
accomplishments she added the playing of the organ.
Though the works of Bach, Mozart and Beethoven
were much loved by Burne-Jones, it was significantly
the sound of an old English tune, perhaps played on a
street-organ outside the house, which moved him as
nothing else could.

It has been said that 'none expressed the Pre-
Raphaelite ideal of art as a way of life better than
Burne-Jones'. Both his home and life-style fed and
complemented his work, which in its turn spilled over
from pure painting into many forms of domestic
decoration as well as drawings and illustrations which
he made for the delight of his many friends and their
children.

CANON VALPY

Canon Valpy, a member of the Chapter of Winchester Cathedral, was a man of considerable private means. He had a butler, two footmen, a groom, a personal maid for his wife and the usual quota of other servants. Like Archdeacon Grantley in Anthony Trollope's novel *The Warden*, his table was laden with solid silver. One can see the same 'comfortable air of all the belongings', as Trollope described Grantley's home, in Corfe's watercolours of Canon Valpy's rooms. But there the comparison ends. Trollope's satirical eye, observing the old china on Grantley's table, 'worth about a pound a piece, but very despicable in the eye of the uninitiated',

would have found little to despise at 3 The Close, Winchester. Here the discrimination and taste with which the Canon and his wife chose their possessions resulted in a pleasant and 'homely' house, which was also elegant in that understated way which is typical of a certain kind of English taste.

Though still eclectic in its furnishings, the house nevertheless had a preponderance of eighteenth-century furniture which, together with the clusters of low-hung watercolours and prints on plain walls, assorted easy-chairs hidden under matching chintz, a few well-chosen ornaments replacing indiscriminate clutter, and piles of books lying around looking as if they were for reading rather than for show, gave the home an appearance more akin to that of the Hardens or the Bosanquets than to houses furnished in the intervening years. Thus Canon Valpy's home marks a revolution in the wheel of taste of the nineteenth century, a taste which has remained popular. There must be many rooms in medium-sized provincial houses today which look remarkably like the Canon's home.

PREVIOUS PAGES *The drawing-room and study* ABOVE LEFT *The dining-room* ABOVE *Mrs Valpy's sitting-room, 3 The Close, Winchester; watercolours by B.O.Corfe, c. 1900. Eighteenth-century taste and nineteenth-century comfort have been happily combined in Canon Valpy's home as genuine Sheraton and Chippendale furniture intermingles with Victorian armchairs. Valpy's taste for eighteenth-century furniture coincided with the Georgian revival at the beginning of the twentieth century. There was a desire for an English style in furniture and decoration, which the Georgian style was considered to be, in reaction to the many foreign influences recently so popular.*

In the drawing-room the easy-chairs are covered in matching chintz and are surrounded by skilfully grouped watercolours hung at eye level to harmonize with the Georgian proportions of the room. The wooden panelling in the study was considered an appropriate background for a masculine domain. The low-backed Windsor chair, known as a 'smoker's bow', was frequently found in studies and smoking-rooms.

ALFRED BROOKS

After their marriage in 1886, Alfred Brooks and his wife moved into Hillside, a house built for them at Grays Thurrock in Essex, by a local architect called Shiner. It was a square, yellow-brick, villa-type house with a kitchen and three rooms on the ground floor and four rooms above. After two children had been born and his fortune increased, Mr Brooks enlarged the house, adding a kitchen and nursery wing, together with a conservatory and boudoir for his wife.

Alfred Brooks was a Quaker and his wife a Wesleyan. Their lives followed a familiar pattern among Nonconformists in the nineteenth century, one which showed a marked compatibility between commercial success and good works. Alfred Brooks's father had pioneered a cement business in Essex and, together with his partner and brother-in-law, had built up a thriving business called Brooks, Shoobridge and Company. When old enough Alfred and his two brothers joined the firm and enlarged it. Alfred ran the works which were close to his home.

Both he and his wife were increasingly active in local affairs and initiated a number of philanthropic projects, such as building a mission hall for his workers. These affairs took a great deal of time, leaving little for social occasions. Mrs Brooks's social life seems largely to have fitted into an 'At Home' day on the first Wednesday of every month. On these days the house was cleaned and polished from top to bottom, the silver cleaned and the best tea-set put out, and Mrs Brooks, dressed in her best tea-gown, would then wait in her drawing-room for her visitors. This was a regular ritual in middle- and upper-class circles almost until the outbreak of the First World War. Everyone had a certain day when it was known that they would be at home to await calls. If one called on the wrong day and the hostess was out, one's card was left on the silver salver in the hall. 'Leaving and returning cards was a solemn ritual . . . omission branded you as a crank or at worst discourteous', wrote Hannah Cohen. Mrs Brooks's monthly Wednesdays and return visits were her chief form of social encounter. For one short period the Brookses had fortnightly weekend tennis parties, but the pressure of charitable commitments brought them to an end.

Their four children, three boys and a girl, lived a day-school and nursery existence until they went to boarding-school when about twelve years old. All the children's meals were taken in the nursery, except for

Detail of a room, Hillside, Grays Thurrock, Essex, 1896. A closed, cast-iron enamelled stove in a carefully designed setting. The geometric patterns and formalized plant forms on the wallpaper and tiles show the influence of Owen Jones and Christopher Dresser.

Sunday lunch and this only when they were considered old enough to have learnt sufficient table-manners to be allowed to eat with their parents in the dining-room.

Everything for the house was chosen because it was of good quality rather than because of any artistic merit it might have had. Some of the furniture was bought in Shoolbred's, where one could completely furnish a room in whichever style one preferred. These included styles designated 'Old English', medieval, Jacobean, Stuart, Adams style (*sic*) and Louis XVI, the latest historical style to be revived. Mrs Brooks's boudoir was furnished from Waring and Gillow and other pieces in the house came from Maples; both Maples and Waring and Gillow were large furnishing stores in London.

Alfred Brooks kept abreast of all the mechanical inventions of the day and had several different cameras. He was a proficient photographer as the photographs which he took of his home show. He owned one of the first Daimlers – which he drove himself; later he was one of the first people to have a gramophone. He was evidently less interested in the arts for there were few paintings in the house apart from his wife's sketches and a number of prints. The ornaments mostly came from his wife's father who had brought them back from India when serving there in the army as a ranker officer. The spinning-chair in the drawing-room was carved by his wife who went to evening classes which she herself had helped

The drawing-room, Hillside, Grays Thurrock, 1896.

set up. Mrs Brooks was also accomplished at singing and playing the piano. The 'Queen Anne' display cabinet at the end of the drawing-room was an example of the aesthetic taste of the 1880s. The white-painted wooden arch in fretwork in the same room was a very popular device in the 1890s for making alcoves or bays or dividing spaces. It was a cheap and easy way of achieving an architectonic effect. Such fittings could be bought ready made in a number of different 'architectural' styles, one of the most popular of which was 'Mooresque'. The importance of the frieze and the disappearance of the dado reflected the new trend towards the simplification of wall decoration. The animal skins used as rugs were a reflection of a fashion in the late 1870s; *The Queen* newspaper gave the curious advice of using them to replace antimacassars on the grounds that 'they wear well, have nothing tawdry about them and never require washing'. Though the Brookses did not profess to be interested in the decorative arts, their house was clearly furnished with considerable care and restraint.

THOMAS SUMMERSON

Thomas Summerson's home was the realization of what must have seemed to him an impossible dream for the first twenty years of his life. While his was not quite a 'rags to riches' story, it was certainly a striking example of how, through the processes of industrialization, an intelligent member of the labouring poor, as working-class people were then called, could rise to the middle class. For Thomas Summerson experienced the Janus face of the industrial revolution: exploitation and opportunity.

He was born in 1811 in South Shields in County Durham, the heart of the coal and iron industry. His family were members of the Church of England. His father made biscuits for ships but the business failed and, when Thomas was eleven years old, the family moved south to West Auckland where Thomas was apprenticed to his uncle, a cobbler. It was the dawn of the railway age and, at fourteen, Thomas went to work in a quarry, drilling stone blocks to be used as sleepers on the Stockton and Darlington Line. He and his fellow workers were, in his own words, 'cruelly used': their wages were 8d per day for a minimum of twenty-four blocks drilled or else the pay was

RIGHT ABOVE *The hall*   FAR RIGHT ABOVE *The larder*   RIGHT BELOW *The dining-room*   FAR RIGHT BELOW *Thomas Summerson's bedroom, his house in Haughton-Le-Skerne, County Durham, c. 1899.*

The hall is typical of many a modest middle-class home: a dark passage-way with a painted dado, a washable floor covering and a row of hat-pegs.

The contents of the larder, including the rubber hot-water bottle hanging on the door, are much the same as one might find in a larder today, apart from the water filter, made by Doulton, on the floor. Such ornamental filters, designed to stand in the dining-room, were a necessity in the 1890s when drinking-water was frequently polluted by the drains flowing into springs and wells.

In the dining-room genuine eighteenth-century chairs of varying styles surround a table carefully covered in protective baize. The heavy, gilt-framed landscape hanging from the cornice pole, and the substantial mahogany furniture give an air of solid respectability.

Summerson's bedroom is a simple room, as one would expect of 'a plain-living man who despised luxury'; the other rooms reflect the taste of his children, overlaying that of Summerson and his wife.

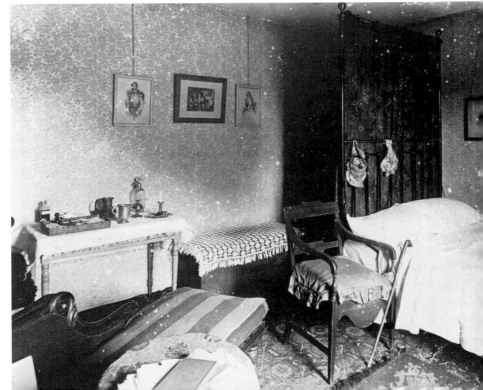

reduced. After the line was opened in 1825 he spent five years at 11s a week oiling and repairing a part of the line. Eventually he became an assistant plate-layer, finally gaining a platelayer's job at 16s a week. After a brief spell working on the construction of the Stanhope and Tyne Railway, he returned to the Stockton and Darlington Line, carrying out various maintenance jobs. In 1836 he went with the engineer, a Mr Storey, to survey for the Great North of England Railway, from Darlington to York. The further they penetrated into the country, the greater grew the opposition from the farmers who feared that their livelihood was being severely threatened. It fell to Thomas Summerson to gain their permission to leave the railwaymen's poles and chains overnight on their land. His quiet, persuasive manner in telling the farmers that the railwaymen were only poor workmen glad to get work and were not to blame won the day. After this he returned to platelaying until, in 1838, he was recommended for the job of inspector of a part of the line. This unsolicited stroke of good fortune turned him overnight into a 'blue-collar' worker. It 'totally changed the current of my life', he wrote, 'as I had never expected being anything but a working man'. For Summerson work meant manual work, as it did for most of society at that time, and thus his promotion raised him out of the working class. Significantly the following year, at the age of twenty-eight, he married, choosing a wife from a background of a higher social standing than his own.

Summerson's fortunes continued to flourish. In 1843 he became a general inspector under John Harris, the engineer of the Stockton and Darlington Line who had succeeded Mr Storey, and he continued in this work for the next ten years, until Harris's contract came to an end. Harris then bought the lease of a foundry at Hopetown and invited Summerson to become his manager. Summerson accepted and combined managing the foundry with organizing a number of railway projects in which Harris was involved. During this period his previous practical experience on the railways led him to introduce certain improvements. It was he who was responsible for replacing those heavy stone blocks with wooden sleepers which soon became universally used. Another invention, which he patented in 1855, was a wheel with a wrought-iron ring inserted inside the trot to prevent it from breaking. The cast-iron wheels of the wagons on the Stockton and Darlington Line broke so frequently that they often brought the service to a halt. The directors sought to remedy this by offering to order 10,000 wheels from anyone who could produce a wheel which could stand up to the traffic. Summerson's invention won him the order and he made them in conjunction with John Harris at the Hopetown foundry. His reputation as an inventor grew and he added to it by inventing the first signal lamp.

Meanwhile his family had also grown. In 1857 he bought a house in the village of Haughton-Le-Skerne in County Durham. This substantial property confirmed his now middle-class status and contained all those appurtenances needed to support a middle-class way of life. The house had seven bedrooms, a dining-room, a drawing-room, two further rooms which were used as nurseries, a kitchen with a large pantry and a deep cellar. Outside was a yard in which stood various outbuildings including a wash-house, a stable big enough for two horses above which was a hay-loft, a coach-house and a pigsty with a room above for the children's pet rabbits and guinea-pigs. An acre of garden stocked with apple and pear trees, and redcurrant, blackcurrant and gooseberry bushes, together with a brick summer-house in which the family entertained their friends and neighbours, completed the homestead. Here Thomas Summerson lived with his wife, four sons and seven daughters.

Through the reminiscences of one of his daughters – who was born in 1853 – it is possible to gain a glimpse into the family home. Her father was 'a nervous, shy man, strong and vigorous, a great walker ... fond of the country having a great love of wild nature'. As might be expected 'he avoided company', as well as 'places of amusement'. It was a close-knit family to the extent that the marriage of a daughter was seen as an irreparable loss rather than a cause for celebration. After the marriage of his twin daughters Thomas Summerson viewed all young men with suspicion, which was a great trial to his still unmarried daughters. When one of his sons died, the parents were inconsolable for a considerable length of time. In contrast to their father their mother was gregarious and fun-loving, far from the image of the stern and strict Victorian parent; as her daughter wrote, 'our pleasures were hers'. Childhood was fun at the house at Haughton-Le-Skerne: sliding on a piece of wood from the top to the bottom of the back stairs, playing marbles or cherrystones on the gravel and lime nursery floor where holes had been specially made for this children's game, eating juicy pears from the garden and sipping home-made wines which their mother brewed were some of the pleasures which the Summerson children enjoyed.

In such a home the children's talents could flourish. The natural intelligence and resourcefulness of Thomas Summerson was to come out in his children and grandchildren, the most illustrious of whom to date is his grandson, the lucid and scholarly architectural historian and writer, Sir John Summerson.

JAMES KITSON

James Kitson's father, also James Kitson (1807–85), like his contemporary Thomas Summerson, was a successful example of the philosophy expressed in Samuel Smiles's book *Self-Help*, published in 1859. An engineering genius, the elder James Kitson progressed from being a licensed victualler to founding and making his fortune from the locomotive industry of Leeds. He took part in the public life of the city, had a large house and educated his sons at University College, London. His elder son died comparatively young but his second son, James, brought further lustre to the family name together with an even greater fortune. With money, education and ambition, the younger James Kitson, like so many sons of self-made men, was able to lead a broader life than his father. He sought a public and political career on a national level, as well as managing to increase his industrial assets.

The right kind of home was an essential part of the equipment for such a life, and in 1885 the younger James bought an elegant eighteenth-century house called Gledhow Hall designed by John Carr of York in 1764. About three miles from the centre of Leeds, it had 150 acres of gardens, parks and farmlands and an appropriately long, circuitous drive, in spite of being set close to the road on one side. This estate was the power-base from which Sir James, as he shortly became, emulated the life-style of the older landed gentry. He extended generous hospitality to his family, to his workers in his iron foundry, to his political friends and acquaintances, as well as to other representatives of causes which he supported. He entertained by giving vast luncheon and tea parties on his lawn. His first wife had died before he moved to Gledhow and his second left him shortly afterwards. His elder daughter Emily, at the age of twenty-three, filled her stepmother's place as her father's hostess. Her housekeeping book dating from 1889 gives valuable glimpses into the scale of her father's entertaining.

The drawing-room, Gledhow Hall, near Leeds, c. 1900. The integral design of the panelled walls and alcove shows a desire to make an architectural unity of the room. This quality is enhanced by the matching chair covers and by the absence of clutter. The ceiling, with its high relief 'Jacobean' pattern, was probably made out of reinforced papier mâché – a popular and cheap device for simulating plasterwork.

In 1889 Sir James entertained sixty foremen from his iron foundry at Monkbridge and Airedale to a sit-down meal on the lawn. They consumed a total of 46lb. of salmon, 17 chickens, 5 tongues, 17lb. of sirloin, 12lb. of ham, 3 veal-and-ham pies, 60 fruit tarts, 40 cheese cakes, 207 bread buns, 6 cakes, 6lb. of tomatoes and 4 cucumbers – the grand cost of which was £14 18s 3d. The amount of alcohol drunk was 11 bottles of hock, 16 bottles of claret, 5 of sherry and 7 of whisky; two boxes of cigars were smoked. To wait on the guests, eight extra servants were hired to help. Less than three weeks later, 340 Leeds women of the Liberal Association were invited to tea and were entertained with a band. Similar entertainments were extended to his Colne Valley constituents whom he represented as a Liberal Member of Parliament for fifteen years.

His private entertaining was just as prodigal. There were frequent dinner parties for sixteen guests at a time; balls for as many as 250 guests; children's dances and fancy-dress parties (there were five Kitson children at Gledhow); great annual Christmas and New Year parties; bachelor parties; tennis and picnic parties; and above all weekend house parties – that particularly Victorian country-house institution. The most important social event in the calendar was the triennial Leeds music festival, for which around nine guests would stay for a week. It must have been with some relief that Emily wrote, after these events, 'most successful party', or 'everything went off satis-

factorily'. All this entertaining was squeezed into less than six or seven months of the year. The rest of the year Kitson spent in his London house, on the Riviera or travelling elsewhere.

An appraisal of Sir James in the *Pall Mall Magazine* described him as leading a simple and patriarchal life among his children, as well as entertaining the leading men of his day. The Kitson family were Unitarians, closely connected with the Mill Hill Chapel where Sir James was a Sunday-school teacher. One descendant of the family has made the point that, although his guests at Gledhow included every Liberal Prime Minister from Gladstone onwards, he entertained many less illustrious people. Family parties for his numerous relations, many of whom were of the solid wealthy society of Leeds, are recorded in Emily's book. One guest who stayed more frequently than anyone else was Herbert Gladstone, who as the Member for Midlothian found Gledhow something of a refuge when visiting his constituency. Not the least part of the attraction was probably Emily herself who was very pretty and intelligent. However, her sense of duty to her father seems to have overruled any passions she may have had, for she never left her father's side.

An insight into how some intelligent Victorian girls such as Emily tried to use their undervalued intellects is given by the Little Owls' Society, a ladies' discussion group in Leeds which met at various members' houses. A member would read a paper on a

ABOVE *The boudoir* ABOVE RIGHT *The dining-room, Gledhow Hall, near Leeds, c. 1900. A characteristic common to many of the rooms at Gledhow (including the study, shown in the frontispiece) is the extensive use of patterned wallpapers which, in many rooms, cover even the ceiling. The practice of dividing the wall into four or five different parts – skirting, dado, 'filling' (the area between the dado and the frieze), frieze and cornice – dated from the 1880s when dados and friezes in particular were considered mandatory when creating an aesthetic interior. In Emily Kitson's boudoir the 'filling' has been covered in an unobtrusive wallpaper which makes a suitable background for the watercolours crammed on the walls. Millais's 'Forget-me-not' hangs in the panelled recess in the dining-room.*

chosen subject which was then discussed. The nine papers written by Emily included subjects with titles such as 'Are Modern Manners Improving?', 'Does the Influence of Women for Good or Evil Preponderate in Shakespeare?', 'The Pre-Raphaelite Movement – its Aims and Works' and 'What Effect has Ruskin's Teaching on our Society?' These discussions, held between 1893 and 1910, were attended by some seventy members.

Gledhow was not a large house in 'stately-home' terms, but it was the grandest of those belonging to the Leeds entrepreneurial circle. It was said that it annoyed Sir James that the rates on Gledhow were higher than those on nearby Harewood, home of the Earls of Harewood; this was because of Gledhow's greater proximity to Leeds where land values were higher. To support his hospitable life-style Kitson had a staff at Gledhow of approximately ten indoor servants. Emily's notebook for 1889 lists their salaries, the highest of which was for Gorman, the butler, who was paid £60 a year. The servants had ten days' holiday annually. Female servants had to be home by 9.00 p.m. on weekdays and 9.30 p.m. on Saturdays. Emily meticulously scheduled their duties, particularly the cleaning tasks of the house-maid. Servants in Victorian houses were most popular when least visible, so the cleaning of the public parts of the house was done when the family and guests were still in their bedrooms, and vice versa; hence the injunction to servants that 'those who would thrive must rise by five'. The arduous task of keeping Victorian houses clean was considered an important matter, particularly since the discovery that 'dust and disease are intimately associated'. At Gledhow, as in many houses by the 1880s, in deference to hygienic precepts, rugs (surrounded by a stained or polished wooden floor) had largely replaced the hitherto ubiquitous fitted carpets. For William Morris, a strong supporter of the change, this was an aesthetic benefit as well as a hygienic one. The health of a house and its 'art' were to him inseparable.

When Sir James bought Gledhow, he employed Chorley and Connor, *the* architects of Leeds at the time, to alter the house. A three-storied wing was added to the north elevation to provide a billiard-room and a large sitting-room on the ground floor and

Design for a bathroom at Gledhow Hall, c. 1885. A Roman-inspired bathroom – the ultimate in luxury.

142

extra sleeping accommodation on the other floors. There were two bathrooms at Gledhow which, by contemporary standards, was quite luxurious. The servants' rooms were in the attic (Gorman, the butler, had his own house) and the view from their windows was restricted by a balustrade which encircled the house. This was a common device to protect the family and friends when they were in the garden from the gaze of their servants. There was no basement at Gledhow and the rooms were disposed round a central hall. The kitchen led off the dining-room. A stained-glass window in the dining-room looking onto the kitchen corridor gave some light, but its high placing in the wall ensured that the servants could not see the family when they were dining. The care that nineteenth-century householders took not to be overlooked or overheard by their servants on the one hand, and their absolute dependence on them on the other, reflected the duality of their relationship. Even John Harden at the beginning of the century preferred to row his guests on Lake Windermere himself rather than have his servants do it as, in his own words, 'we are free of the presence of servants and consequently of some restraint of conversation, are more independent in our enjoyments and fully our own masters. . . .'

After the alterations at Gledhow little of Carr's interior decorative work remained. In the dining-room it was replaced by a pseudo-Jacobean carved dado and panelled recess, together with a riot of different wallpapers. A galaxy of both oil and electric lights hung from the ceiling, and dark reproduction or pseudo eighteenth-century furniture – some of it possibly genuine – completed the room's sombre masculine look. Flowers on the sideboard and side-table were to decorate each place-setting on the dining-table; this custom replaced the earlier one of using silver epergnes. Ruskin recommended the use of flowers for 'taking away the animal look of eating'. The most charming object in the room was the painting by Millais called *Forget-me-not*. The sitter was Millais's daughter, Effie, and Sir James bought the painting because she looked so like Emily. Sir James's study and Emily's boudoir housed their personal treasures, leaving the white drawing-room, with its 'Jacobean' ceiling, devoid of clutter. The demise of clutter was a growing trend, coincidental with the emergence of electric lighting under whose bright and relentless glare the dust and tawdriness of objects was shown up, considerably lessening their appeal. Though Gledhow lost its genuine eighteenth-century decorations it was, nevertheless, more restrained and less pretentious in its interior decoration and furniture than many other houses belonging to men of similar fortunes and backgrounds as Sir James. It was said of him that 'everything about him spells solidity and endurance'. Gledhow reflected the solidity of its owner: it was a home rather than a showpiece.

MODEST HOMES

The homes of the poor in Victorian England provide a dramatic contrast to those of the middle and upper classes whose houses and life-styles have been described in the preceding pages. The simplicity and squalor of some working men's homes were evidence of the great gulf which divided this class from other sections of society.

RURAL COTTAGES

Rural cottages seldom corresponded to their idyllic pastoral image: too often they were miserable slums with damp and semi-putrid walls, leaky roofs, infected rooms and deficient sleeping space. These were the legacies of badly-built houses – the fault in the first place of uncharitable parishes and speculative builders but made worse by the failure of landlords to make repairs. They became a category of home which, as one report put it, was 'deficient in almost every requisite that should constitute a home for a Christian family in a civilized community'. This comment was made nearly thirty years after the Society for Improving the Conditions of the Labouring Classes had been established in 1844 under the patronage of Queen Victoria and Prince Albert, with Lord Shaftesbury as President. However, an awakening of social conscience, together with the more pragmatic view that poor accommodation hastened the farmworkers' drift to the towns, had combined by 1857 to make the subject of farm cottages at least a common topic of conversation.

Plenty of advice was given as to what should constitute a model cottage and, in spite of many regional differences affecting materials, there was a consensus on a number of points. But the issue which eventually led to improvement was, not surprisingly, a moral one. Cottages had frequently been built without any divisions of space and the kitchen usually had two beds along the back wall. The growing conviction in Victorian England that the sexes should be separated led to the building of bed-closets – small confined areas leading off the kitchen for which it was recommended that landlords should furnish brass beds suitable in size for only one occupant. The closet was considered to retain all the advantages of having beds in the kitchen, namely the use of fire for heat and light, with the additional ones of a door to shut it off from the kitchen and a window to ventilate it. Sometimes a bed was left in the kitchen for parents with room for a crib to stand next to it. In two-storied cottages beds were usually removed from the ground floor and the upper rooms designated for sleeping.

Though improvement associations tried to prevent overcrowding, the largest cottages were never built with more than three sleeping rooms, which for a big family was scarcely ample. However, as Flora Thompson explained in her book, *Lark Rise to Candleford*, an evocation of her childhood in the 1880s beginning in the hamlet she called Lark Rise in North Oxfordshire, families managed: by the time the last baby was born the oldest children were usually away at work, so the whole family was seldom in the house at once. Overcrowding was more often caused by rents being too high, so forcing the family to take in lodgers. Larger cottages generally had two rooms on the ground floor and a small scullery and pantry. The second room was occasionally turned into the proverbial parlour, that 'dreary and useless' room as William Morris described it. It was sometimes recommended that cottages be built without back doors because of complaints that they made the house cold. Even in model cottages the cold persisted, as one occupant complained: 'Sit where I like, I always have a cold wind in my back, so that when I am roasting before, I am starving behind, for I canna turn aboot but my back is either sticking into a door or a window.'

Sanitation in most cottages remained crude. Few labourers were fortunate enough to have cottages built by someone like Harriet Martineau, who

A house in Conway; detail of watercolour by W.J.Müller, 1839. The occupants of this once grand house were the forerunners of today's squatters. Traditionally squatters were peasants who built themselves simple huts on waste land.

installed privies each with its own patent water-closet apparatus. Most had the same rudimentary arrangements as the cottages in Lark Rise in the 1880s. A small, beehive-shaped building, universally called the hovel, was erected in either the corner of a shed or the garden. In it a deep pit was dug and covered with a seat. In Flora Thompson's cottage the pit was

Cottage interior by Myles Birket-Foster, c. 1880.

emptied once a year, but in many other places this was not done: when it became full another pit was dug alongside. Leaving sewage in the soil frequently led to contaminated water supplies, or poisonous gases invading the home. Some privies were clean and decent and some were horrible holes. As Flora Thompson said, they were often a reflection of the characters of their owners.

The interiors of cottages varied as much. At best they were like the Welsh farmhouse (opposite) which most nearly corresponded to the pastoral ideal. It exemplifies what William Morris called 'the simplicity of life, begetting simplicity of taste'. There were other country areas where the peasantry could similarly pride themselves on their 'cleanliness and propriety'. The Norwich peasantry was said to do so, despite the poverty which accompanied wages of only 8s or 10s a week. They, like the Welsh, were said to have 'showed a degree of taste manifested by the chimney ornament . . . and the table coverlet'.

The hearth was the centre of life and was probably lit all the year round. In Wales this was a symbol of the perpetuation of family life. The fire as a focus for domestic life has been a characteristic common to all the homes described in this book. This has been described as an 'Atlantic' custom as opposed to a 'European' one, for on the Continent it was the table and not the hearth which was the social focus. In Britain the best seat in the house was always that nearest the fire, occupied by the head of the family and only relinquished when a guest was present.

Food was traditionally cooked in a pot suspended on a large hook over the fire. Sometimes a baking oven was let into the wall alongside the fireplace. If not, the bread was baked in a 'pot oven' which was placed in the fire and covered with glowing peat, simulating the conditions of a closed oven. A third method of baking bread was in a closed pot hung over the fire in the traditional manner.

In Birket-Foster's drawing of a corner of a cottage whose occupant shares it with chickens and firewood, one sees a great contrast to the Welsh farmhouse.

'Miserable abodes' like this remained a fact of life throughout the nineteenth century: 'The decent cottage was the exception – the hovel the rule.'

COTTAGES IN MINING AREAS

The inadequacies which rural cottages suffered from were shared by those which lined the narrow lanes and filthy alleys of most industrial towns, but the latter had the additional disadvantage that their inhabitants lived under a pall of black soot making day almost indistinguishable from night.

In a typical pit village there were three sizes of cottage: those with two rooms on the ground floor, those with one room on the ground floor and a loft

Interior of a Welsh farmhouse; watercolour by G.P. Yeats, c. 1870. Homes like this were a source of inspiration to such nineteenth-century architects as Norman Shaw in their rediscovery of the vernacular. Traditional features include an ingle-nook with a settle, wooden trenchers, pewter plates for use on special occasions, a hanging chain from which to suspend the cooking-pot, and an oak table.

above, and those with two rooms below and a loft above. Pit cottages were generally built in pairs and stood in rows. Paired cottages had the advantage of being warmer and drier than single ones, though neither of these factors was a problem for the coal

ABOVE *Cottage in Northumberland, c. 1900. Over the hearth is a chimney-crane with an assortment of ratten crooks from which to suspend the cooking-pots.*
RIGHT *The unchanging bed-sitter: the lodging of the poet Robert Bloomfield in London; watercolour by Thomas Wykeham Archer, 1850.*

miner as the one thing which he did have was plenty of cheap or even free coal. The houses had no privies so dunghills were used outside the back doors. Each row of cottages was provided with a large oven for the use of all the inhabitants. It has been suggested that the association of the working-class communal oven with baking was the reason for the middle- and upper-class prejudice against baking as being an inferior method of cooking, even though it was recommended as a more efficient and economic method than roasting.

LODGINGS

A number of cheap lodging-houses, some for men and some for women, were built in cities by improvement associations, the aim being to 'provide comfortable cheap and healthy abodes free from vice and immorality, which beset the inmates of a crowded cottage. . . .' Such lodgings were run by a superintendent and the lodgers slept in dormitories subdivided into rooms about 8 feet by 5 feet, with a window, bed, flap-table, stool and locker or clothes box, and costing 2d a day. The rules were strict: no spirits or card-playing, and smoking only in the kitchen.

THE REVEREND ROBERT HAY COATS

The year 1901 marked the end of Victorian England. Appropriately, the new home of the young Revd Robert Hay Coats was furnished and decorated in the new style that pioneered modern design. Coats was born in Paisley, a member of the famous thread family of the same name. He was educated at Glasgow and Oxford Universities where he obtained degrees in divinity and the arts. His wife was the daughter of a leading Glasgow lawyer called John MacConnachie. Shortly before her marriage she had visited the Glasgow Exhibition of 1901 where she saw the work of the designer and painter Ernest Read Taylor, and was greatly impressed. As a wedding present, her father provided her with the means to build a house and to commission Taylor to furnish and decorate it. The house was designed by the architects Gately and Parsons and was built at Handsworth, near Birmingham, where Robert Coats was to take up his first Baptist ministry. Correspondence between Coats and Taylor relating to the latter's work on the house, together with a number of bills for the furniture, still exist.

Taylor was one of a group of Glasgow designers influenced by Charles Rennie Mackintosh, the great Art Nouveau architect and designer. Art Nouveau was the name of the style which derived its inspiration from forms and shapes found in nature; it was an attempt to free design from continual recourse to historical styles. In England the movement was generated by designers and architects such as A.H. Mackmurdo and C.F.A. Voysey. It was also a part of the Arts and Crafts movement which developed from Morris's principle of the artist-craftsman as designer and maker, in opposition to the factory system with its machine-made products. Taylor, who designed for the Glasgow firm of furnishers, Wylie and Lochhead, had absorbed the ethics of the Arts and Crafts movement and combined them with the style of Art Nouveau. In his work for the Coatses, this resulted in the simplification of the interior and an attempt to make an artistic unity not only of each room, but also in the relationship of one room to another – a prelude to the Modern Movement. Coincident with trying to make a harmonious whole was the rejection of arbitrary clutter which had characterized so many Victorian homes in the previous thirty years. Though Taylor's interiors were more moderate and reticent than Mackintosh's, of which Hermann Muthesius said, 'Even a book in an unsuitable binding would

disturb the atmosphere simply by lying on the table', their aims of paring down and simplifying were the same. These aims conformed, as Muthesius also observed, with a preference for 'hygiene' rather than 'the sumptuousness and cosiness of the old style'. His prescient forecast that the concepts of health and beauty, in relation to design and decoration, would become identical was soon to be evidenced in the white walls, flush surfaces and built-in furniture of the Modern Movement. The exhortation made by Voysey, 'Begin by casting out all the useless ornaments and remove the dust catching furbelows . . . to produce an effect of repose and simplicity', began to be heeded. However, such formulae did not become universal; homes continued to differ as much in the new century as they had in the preceding one.

ABOVE LEFT *The dining-room* ABOVE *The hall* RIGHT *The sitting-room, the Coatses' house at Handsworth, near Birmingham, 1901. E.R.Taylor's austerely simple interiors contain the seeds of the Modern Movement. Here, however, they have been unhappily fused with the Tudor revival, to be seen in the hall in the half-timbered ceiling and 'olde' lantern.*

NOTES

NOTES are related to their text by the page number on which the relevant text appears and by the first few words of the quotation (in quotation marks) or of author's text (without quotation marks) to which the note refers. Full biographical details are given only the first time a source is mentioned.

JOHN HARDEN

Quotations in this section not attributed to other sources come from Jessy Harden's unpublished Journals, 1804–11, in the possession of the Abbot Hall Art Gallery, Kendal.

There are over 300 drawings and watercolours by John Harden in the Abbot Hall Gallery. A.S. Clay, a great-grandson of Harden, says that his grandmother had 1,600 and that there were also a number of drawings owned by descendants of Harden's brother.

p.25   'a white palace'. S.T. Coleridge, November 1798. Quoted in Daphne Foskett, *John Harden of Brathay Hall* (Abbot Hall Art Gallery, Kendal 1974), p. 19.

p.25   'There are two words'. Don Manuel Alvarez Espriella, *Letters from England*, translated by Robert Southey, 3 vols. (London 1807). Vol. I, p. 180. Espriella was an imaginary traveller invented by Southey.

p.29   'I grieve to say'. Jessie Harden's unpublished Diary, 1842–3, in the Abbot Hall Art Gallery.

p.29   Lord Lansdowne at his house. Arnold Palmer, *Movable Feasts* (London and New York 1952), p. 54.

p.29   'still dining at 4.00'. Jessie Harden's Diary.

p.31   'I love large'. C.B. Andrews (Ed.), *The Torrington Diaries containing the tours through England & Wales of the Hon. John Byng, later Fifth Viscount Torrington, between the years 1781 and 1784* (London 1930), Vol. III, pp. 156–7. Entry for 3 July 1792.

p.33   the most notable reformer. Sarah Thompson, Countess Rumford, *The Complete Works of Count Rumford* (New York 1870).

p.33   'where comfort and culture'. Essay on 'Culture' in R.W. Emerson, *The Conduct of Life* (New York 1860).

THE DRUMMOND FAMILY

p.34   'one of the noblest'. Sir James Balfour Paul (Ed.), *The Scots Peerage*, Vol. VIII (Edinburgh 1911), p. 225.

p.34   founded ... Drummonds Bank. Hector Bolitho and Derek Peel, *The Drummonds of Charing Cross* (London 1967).

p.34   transcribed into an album. The Drummond Album, in the possession of Mrs Fenton, a descendant of the Drummonds.

p.37   The accomplishments of the drawing-room. Hannah More, *Strictures on the Modern System of Female Education with a View of the Principles and Conduct among Women of Rank and Fortune*, 2 vols. (London 1799). 5th ed., Vol. I, p. 107.

p.37   'Their knowledge'. More, Vol. II, p. 1.

p.37   'Religion ... should mingle'. Drummond Album.

p.37   'the root of all evil'. Maria and R.L. Edgeworth, *Essays on Practical Education*, 3 vols. (London 1798). Vol. 1, p. 239.

p.41   confirmed the idea. Gordon Rattray Taylor, *The Angel Makers* (London 1958).

p.44   This led to their. Philip Aries, *Centuries of Childhood* (London 1962).

p.44   'that they might never'. Drummond Album.

THE BOSANQUETS

Charlotte Bosanquet's albums of drawings and watercolours are in the Ashmolean Museum, Oxford.

p.45   'nothing gives a room'. Mrs Loudon (Ed.), *Cottage, Farm* and Villa Architecture and Furniture, the late J.C. Loudon (London 1846), pp. 798–9. This was a new edition of J.C. Loudon's *Encyclopaedia of Cottage, Farm and Villa Architecture* (London 1833).

p.45 'tables, sofas'. E.T. Joy, 'Furniture' in R. Edwards and L.G.G. Ramsey (Eds.), *Connoisseur Period Guides: The Regency Period* (London 1958), p. 39.

p.45 'improved modes'. Mrs Loudon, p. 1072.

p.52 'The comedy was'. A.E. Richardson, 'Architecture' in G.M. Young (Ed.), *Early Victorian England 1830–65* (London 1951) Vol. II, p. 241.

TOWN HOUSE

p.57 'indiscriminate borrowings'. Peter Floud, 'Furniture' in *Connoisseur Period Guides: The Early Victorian Period 1830–60*, R. Edwards and L.G.C. Ramsay (Eds.) (London 1958), p. 38.

p.57 Chairs similar to Lawfords. Reproduced in *Pictorial Dictionary of British 19th Century Furniture Design*, with an introduction by Edward Joy (Antique Collectors Club, Woodbridge, Suffolk 1977).

p.57 One aspect of rococo. Hans Sedlmayr, Catalogue for 'The Age of Rococo' Exhibition (Munich 1958).

QUEEN VICTORIA

Queen Victoria's Journal. Lord Esher made a typescript from a part of the original manuscript of Queen Victoria's Journal before Princess Beatrice edited her mother's Journal and destroyed the original. It is interesting to compare Princess Beatrice's version with the typescript covering the same period (July 1832 to February 1840): all the Queen's sharp observations and pithy comments, especially concerning her difficult relationship with her mother, the Duchess of Kent, have been deleted by Princess Beatrice who, through her editing, has presented her mother as she no doubt felt she should have been rather than how she was. Quotations in this book from the typescript of the original manuscript are marked QV Journal T; those from the edited version, QV Journal. RA refers to the Royal Archives at Windsor.

p.61 'born and bred there'. RA QV Journal T, 13 July 1837.

p.61 'Claremont remains'. A.C. Benson and Viscount Esher (Eds.), *The Letters of Queen Victoria 1837–61*, 3 vols. (London 1907). Vol. I, p. 14.

p.61 'the dear place'. RA QV Journal, 23 May 1840.

p.61 'it requires all'. Hon. Mrs Hugh Wyndham (Ed.), *Correspondence of Sarah Spencer, Lady Lyttelton*

p.62 *1787–1870* (London 1912), p. 300. 2 October 1840.

p.62 'was the smallest party'. RA QV Journal, 22 April 1842.

p.62 *'Das Landleben'*. Wyndham, p. 300. 2 October 1840.

p.62 'BORING CLAREMONT'. Ibid., p. 337. 8 March 1843.

p.63 'they should be'. J. Mordaunt Crook, *The History of the King's Works* (Gen. Ed. H.M. Colvin), Vol. VI 1782–1851 (London 1973), p. 190.

p.63 Lord Uxbridge. Vera Watson, *A Queen at Home* (London 1952), pp. 42–4.

p.63 'It was a curiously built'. RA QV Journal T, 27 January 1838.

p.64 At Windsor. Ibid., 7 January 1838.

p.64 'We were nearly'. RA QV Journal, 8 December 1843.

p.67 According to Baron Stockmar. Max Muller (Ed.), *Memoirs of Baron Stockmar by his son Baron E. Stockmar*, Vol. II (London 1972), p. 117.

p.68 'required size'. Lord Chamberlain's Reports 1846–50, LC 11/134, Public Record Office.

p.69 One of the more curious. Ibid., 1856.

p.69 twelve hundred were ordered. Ibid., 1860.

p.69 'I cannot help'. RA QV Journal T, 22 August 1837.

p.69 constantly referring. Winslow Ames, *Prince Albert and Victorian Taste* (London 1967), p. 22.

p.69 '£65,000 worth'. Wyndham, p. 280. 5 October 1838.

p.69 'the need for grandeur'. John Cornforth, 'Queen Victoria at Home' in *Country Life*, 26 May 1977.

p.69 'we have succeeded'. Benson and Esher (Eds.), *Letters of Queen Victoria*, Vol. II 1844–53, p. 41. Queen Victoria to Leopold, King of the Belgians, 25 March 1845.

p.69 'we were so occupied'. Ibid., p. 41. Queen Victoria to Lord Melbourne, 3 April 1845.

p.70 opinion of Sir James Clark. Mrs Steuart Erskine (Ed.), *Twenty Years at Court 1842–62. Letters of the Hon. Eleanor Stanley* (London 1916), p. 67.

p.70 'any cottage-looking thing'. Ibid., p. 68.

p.70 'delightfully private'. RA QV Journal, 15 October 1844.

p.70 'the house'. Ibid., 30 March 1845.

p.70 'the rooms are small'. Ibid., 15 October 1844.

p.70 'simple rosewood furniture'. Ibid., 19 June 1845.

p.70 'our *very* own'. Ibid., 20 June 1845.

p.75 '*We dressed early*'. Ibid., 19 November 1857.

p.75 'It is delightful'. Ibid., 19 July 1845.

p.75 'On entering the Hall'. Ibid., 14 September 1846.

p.76 'expanding middle classes'. Catalogue of the House of Oetzmann, 1848–1948, RIBA Library.

p.76 'accessibility and a relaxing'. Elizabeth Longford. *Queen*

Victoria. Born to Succeed (New York 1964), p. 212.

p.76　'it seems like'. RA QV Journal, 15 August 1849.

p.76　So a new Balmoral. C. Woodham-Smith, *Queen Victoria : Her Life and Times* (London 1972), Vol. I, pp. 277–8.

p.77　More Scottish allusions. Ames, p. 104.

p.77　'Every private house'. Victor Mallet (Ed.), *Life with Queen Victoria* (London 1968), p. xix.

p.77　'The small Germanic kingdom'. Ames, p. 106.

THE MELBOURNE–COWPER–PALMERSTON CIRCLE

p.79　'normal life'. David Cecil, *The Young Melbourne* (London 1939), p. 6.

p.80　'housewifely occupations'. Lady Cowper to Frederick Lamb, 25 October (no year). Panshanger Papers, Hertfordshire County Record Office.

p.80　'Here I am ruralizing'. Tresham Lever (Ed.), *The Letters of Lady Palmerston* (London 1957), pp. 37 and 66.

p.80　'I cannot bear'. Mabel, Countess of Airlie, *Lady Palmerston and her Times*, 2 vols. (London 1922). Vol. I, p. 83.

p.80　'small but very cheerful'. RA QV Journal T.

p.82　'were quite delighted'. Queen Victoria to Lady Jocelyn, quoted in Lever, p. 255.

p.82　'could not sit'. Lytton Strachey and Robert Fulford (Eds.), *The Greville Memoirs 1814–60*, Vol. II (London 1938), p. 105.

p.82　Other guests. Both Lady Granville and Princess de Lieven complained of the discomforts of Panshanger. See Lever, pp. 120 and 179.

p.82　'scorched on one side'. *Letters from England*, trans. by Southey, Vol. III, p. 98.

p.82　open fires. Mark Girouard, *The Victorian Country House*, 2nd ed. (Oxford 1971), p. 16. Quoting J.J. Stevenson.

p.82　'The Hollands, at whose home.' Strachey and Fulford, Vol. II, p. 45.

p.83　'exerted herself'. Lady Cowper to Frederick Lamb, n.d., Panshanger Papers.

p.83　On one occasion Princess de Lieven. Lever, p. 185.

p.83　'twenty-six people'. Ibid., p. 144.

p.83　'a very handsome supper'. Ibid., p. 24.

p.83　'little children'. Ibid., p. 63.

p.83　The nursery was ruled. Mabel, Countess of Airlie, *In Whig Society* (London 1921), p. 193.

p.83　'a shining example'. Philip Whitwell Wilson (Ed.), *The Greville Diary*, Vol. II (London 1922), p. 53. Entry for January 1832.

p.84　'furiously Protestant'. Ibid., p. 307. 1850.

p.84　'the fashion'. Lady Cowper to Frederick Lamb, 25 October (no year). Panshanger Papers.

p.84　'*Coopers* enough'. Hon. Mrs Hugh Wyndham (Ed.), *Correspondence of Sarah Spencer, Lady Lyttelton, 1787–1870* (London 1912). Letter dated 28 February 1839.

p.84　'Stay! We will have a party'. F.E. Baily, *Love Story of Lady Palmerston* (London 1938), p. 140.

p.84　her Saturday evening. W. Baring Pemberton, *Lord Palmerston* (London 1954), p. 82.

p.85　'Emily [was] happy'. Lord Palmerston's Diary, Broadlands MSS, Royal Commission on Historic Manuscripts. (By permission of the Trustees of the Broadlands Archives Trust.)

p.86　'I am very comfortable'. Lever, p. 224.

p.86　There were always. Airlie, *Lady Palmerston*.

p.86　Personally interested. Jasper Ridley, *Lord Palmerston* (London 1954).

p.88　even when over seventy. Palmerston's Diary.

p.88　'talked very agreeably'. RA QV Journal T. 29 October 1837.

p.88　The friendship was. John Lewis Bradley (Ed.), *The Letters of John Ruskin to Lord and Lady Mount-Temple* (Ohio State University 1964).

p.88　'no house ever kept'. E.C. Clifford, *Broadlands As It Was* (London 1890), p. 2.

p.88　'had made dear'. Lever, pp. 253–4. Lady Cowper to Frederick Lamb.

p.88　'the house has'. RA QV Journal, 30 July 1841.

THE DUCHESS OF KENT

p.89　'was a very sad'. RA Duchess of Kent's Journal, 15 April 1840. The original manuscript is in the Royal Archives, Windsor Castle.

p.89　according to Nash's estimate. Public Record Office, Work 19/24/1 Clarence House. Letter from John Nash to the Surveyor of the Office of Works.

p.90　A further £14,000. Public Record Office, Work 19/24/1 Clarence House. Letter from Lord Duncannon to the Lords Commissioner of Her Majesty's Treasury.

p.90　'good resolutions'. RA Duchess of Kent's Journal, 21 April 1841.

p.90　'very nice and comfortable'. Ibid., 19 October 1841.

p.90　a partial inventory. Public Record Office, Work 19/24/1.

p.90 'infinite care'. Mark Girouard, *Life in the English Country House* (Yale 1978), p. 276.

p.90 The rooms were furnished. Public Record Office, Work 19/24/1.

p.90 *The Queen* newspaper. *The Queen*, 18 November 1876.

p.93 Mr Seabrook. RA QV Journal, 16 March 1861.

p.93 It had been given. Public Record Office, Work 19/33/1.

p.93 Built in the 1690s. T. Eustace Harwood, *Windsor Old and New* (London 1929).

p.93 The red brick. Anthony Dale, *James Wyatt* (Oxford 1956), p. 181.

p.94 'We lived in a very simple'. Benson and Esher, *Letters of Queen Victoria*, Vol. I, pp. 17–18.

p.94 After Princess Augusta's death. Public Record Office, Work 19/33/1.

p.94 The Queen bought. RA QV Journal, 6 April 1841.

p.94 The servants. Public Record Office, Work 19/33/1.

p.94 less than two years. RA Duchess of Kent's Journal, 19 April 1843.

p.94 'I must say'. Ibid., 26 July 1841.

p.95 'occupied too much'. Ibid., 19 November 1842.

p.95 The Queen did not read. RA QV Journal T, 9 January 1838.

p.96 One lady. Dorothy Wise (Ed.), *Diary of William Tayler, Footman, 1837* (London 1962).

p.96 'not to be'. RA Duchess of Kent's Journal, 26 August 1843.

p.96 'It was too much'. Ibid., 30 August 1850.

p.96 'The subject still'. Ibid., 3 June 1852.

p.96 'put out'. Ibid., 1 December 1841.

p.96 Thirty years' later. *The Queen*, 1876.

Transcripts of Crown-copyright records in the Public Record Office appear by permission of the Controller of H.M. Stationery Office.

GEORGE SCHARF
Sources for George Scharf are his diaries, 1845–95, and his father's notebooks, 1837–59, both in the National Portrait Gallery, London.

WILLIAM KENRICK
Information about William Kenrick comes from R.A. Church, *Kenricks in Hardware* (Newton Abbot 1969).

p.104 In the same year. Barbara Morris, 'The Ante-Room from the Grove at Harborne', *Victoria and Albert Museum Bulletin* (Vols. III and IV, 1967–8). Vol. IV, No. 3, p. 82.

p.104 'elegance and importance'. Quoted in Girouard's *The Victorian Country House*, p. 131.

p.105 'a perfect synthesis'. Morris, 'The Ante-Room from the Grove'.

p.105 'built to be lovely'. John Ruskin, *The Seven Lamps of Architecture* (London 1849).

SAMUEL MONTAGU
p.106 Lancaster Gate. N. Pevsner, *The Buildings of England*, Vol. II (London 1952), p. 308.

p.106 whose rateable value. M.I. Robinson, 'A Study in Urban Growth and Social Patterns' (1979). Unpublished thesis in Marylebone Library, London.

p.106 A countess, a marquis. Court Directory (London 1876).

p.106 he chose Ellen Cohen. C. Bermant, *The Cousinhood. The Anglo-Jewish Gentry* (London 1971), p. 201.

p.107 Mr Barnet. Census of 1871.

p.107 'rage for house'. *The Queen*, 16 December 1876.

p.107 'art' furniture. Charles Eastlake used the term 'artistic furniture' in his third article. 'Hints on Household Taste', written under the pseudonym Jack Easel for *The Queen*, 15 July 1875.

p.107 *A Plea for Art*. W.J. Loftie, *A Plea for Art in the House* (London 1876).

p.107 Mark Pattinson. *The Architect*, 25 November 1876.

p.108 'European idea'. O. Impey, *Chinoiserie* (Oxford 1977), p. 9.

p.108 'if you make any'. 'Luxury in House Decoration' in the *Saturday Review*, 7 September 1878.

p.108 collection of English silver. *The Jewish Chronicle*, 20 January 1911.

p.108 He was typical. Bermant, p. 206. Samuel Montagu became a member of the Burlington Fine Arts Club and the Society of Antiquaries. He became a Liberal M.P. in 1885, a baronet in 1894 and was raised to the peerage in 1907, becoming the first Baron Swaythling.

'THE CLIQUE'
p.111 'authors, artists'. Alan Montgomery Eyre, *Saint John's Wood* (London 1913), p. 37.

p.111 'congenial gloom'. 'Art in the Dining-Room' in the *Saturday Review*, 12 January 1878.

p.111 'to act as a powerful'. Alfred Jowers, 'Interior Decoration of Buildings' in *The House Furnisher and Decorator*, 10 April 1873, p. 47.

THE PRINCE OF WALES

p.113 'If you can imagine'. Dean of Windsor and Hector Bolitho (Eds.), *Letters of Lady Augusta Stanley 1849–63* (London 1927), p. 215.

p.113–15 Sources for the state of Marlborough House come from the Public Record Office. Work 19/18/1.

p.116 The description of the Prince of Wales's day is based mainly on *The Private Life of the King* by one of His Majesty's Servants (London 1901).

p.116 Everything was designed. Philip Magnus, *The Prince of Wales* (London 1964).

GEORGE HYDE WOLLASTON

p.117 Its houses were mainly. Andrew Gomme, Michael Jenner and Brian Little, *Bristol: An Architectural History* (London 1979).

EDWARD BURNE-JONES

The artist is referred to throughout the text as Burne-Jones and his wife, Georgiana, as Lady Burne-Jones, although he did not add Burne to his name until the 1860s and was not made a baronet until 1894.

p.119 'emancipated from stucco'. William Morris in an address to the Trade Guilds of Learning, quoted in the *Saturday Review*, 2 March 1878.

p.119 'a beautiful garden'. G.B.J. (Georgiana Burne-Jones), *Memorials of Edward Burne-Jones*, Vol. I, 1833–67 (London 1904), p. 307.

p.119 'as good in its finish'. *A Brief Sketch of the Morris Movement* (privately printed for the firm of Morris & Co Ltd, 1911).

p.120 Angela Thirkell . . . recalls. Angela Thirkell, *Three Houses* (London 1936), p. 19.

p.120 'good and honest'. *Brief Sketch of the Morris Movement*.

p.121 'You remember'. Lady Mount-Temple, '*M.T.*' *Memorials* (privately printed, 1890), p. 55.

p.121 'attempting to form'. Jack Easel (Charles Eastlake), 'The Fashion for Furniture' in the *Cornhill Magazine*, Vol. IX, No. 51 (1894), pp. 337–49.

p.122 'scarcely deserve'. Review of W.J.Loftie's *A Plea for Art in the House* in *The Architect*, Vol. XVI, 9 December 1876, p. 338.

p.122 'John Bull's comfort'. John Ruskin, under the pseudonym of Kata Phusin, 'Poetry of Architecture' in *The Architectural Magazine and Journal*, Vol. IV, 1837.

p.122 'that in an age of sofas'. G.B.J., p. 59.

p.122 'the only comfortable'. Thirkell, p. 64.

p.122 'I wish London'. This and further quotations in this section not attributed to other sources come from a transcript by Georgiana Burne-Jones of Rooke's Notes which is privately owned. There is a photocopy of a typescript of Rooke's Notes (London 1900) in the Victoria and Albert Museum, London.

p.124 Morris was. M. Harrison and B. Waters, *Burne-Jones* (London 1973), p. 45.

p.124 Jane Alice . . . kept the records. 'Record of the Secret Society', British Museum, Add. MS. 45346.

p.125 'as far as we could'. G.B.J., Vol. II, p. 90.

p.125 The best testimony. Rudyard Kipling, *Something of Myself* (London 1937), p. 11.

p.125 'I have been wanting'. G.B.J., Vol. II, p. 111.

p.126 the help of W.A.S. Benson. W. Benson sold the articles which he designed and made in his shop at 83 New Bond Street. He was an admirer of William Morris's teachings and collaborated with him on a number of schemes. He also designed the garden studio for Burne-Jones and the alterations to his house at Rottingdean. He was the model for Burne-Jones's painting of *King Cophetua and the Beggarmaid*. After Morris died, Benson became chairman of William Morris & Co. Decorators Ltd.

p.126 'none expressed'. Penelope Marcus (Ed.), *Burne-Jones*, Catalogue for Burne-Jones Exhibition (London 1975).

CANON VALPY

Information about Canon Valpy given by Mrs Kingsley Covington.

p.129 'comfortable air'. Anthony Trollope, *The Warden* (London 1855). Chapter 8.

p.129 'worth about a pound'. Ibid.

ALFRED BROOKS

p.131 Alfred Brooks's father. Major A.J. Francis, *Cement Industry 1796–1914*, 2nd ed. (London 1978).

p.131 'Leaving and returning'. Hannah F. Cohen, *Changing Faces – a Memoir of Louisa, Lady Cohen* (London 1937).

p.133 'they wear well'. *The Queen*, 16 December 1876.

THOMAS SUMMERSON

The details of Thomas Summerson's career and family life are based on a transcript of a memorandum by Thomas Summerson (1810–98) – 'Rough biographical sketch of my life', and on a memorandum by Thomas Summerson's daughter, Mrs Wadham

(1853–1953), both in the possession of Sir John Summerson.

JAMES KITSON

p.138 Kitson progressed. 'The Kitsons of Leeds' in *Fortune Made in Business*, Vol. III (London 1887), p. 321. James Kitson Sr. founded Kitson & Co, *c*. 1835. In 1887 the company was turning out 150 locomotives and 50 tramway engines a year. James Kitson Jr. was raised to the peerage before his death.

p.138 150 acres. Will and Codicil of the Rt.Hon. James, Baron Airedale, 1909. Kitson Papers, Leeds Record Office.

p.138 Her housekeeping book. The Hon. Emily Kitson's Notebook, 1889–90. Leeds Record Office.

p.140 Less than three weeks. Ibid.

p.140 'most successful party'. Ibid.

p.140 Little Owls' Society. Kitson Papers.

p.142 'those who would thrive'. Samuel and Sarah Smiles, *The Complete Servant* (London 1825), p. 286.

p.142 'dust and disease'. Robert Edis, *Decoration and Furniture of Town Houses* (London 1881).

p.142 For William Morris. William Morris, *Hopes and Fears for Art* (London 1882), p. 132. Five lectures delivered in Birmingham and Nottingham 1878–81.

p.143 'we are free'. Jessy Harden's Journals.

p.143 'taking away'. John Ruskin, quoted by Revd. Fred Wagstaff FRMS in *House and Home*, Vols. III and IV (1880), p. 61.

p.143 'everything about him'. *Pall Mall Magazine*, quoted in the Kitson Papers.

MODEST HOMES

p.144 'deficient in almost'. Edward Smith, *The Peasant's Home, 1760–1875* (London 1876), p. 6.

p.144 combined by 1857. *Third Annual Report of the Directors of the Association for the Improvement in the Dwellings and Domestic Condition of Agricultural Labourers in Scotland* (Edinburgh 1857).

p.145 as Flora Thompson explained. Flora Thompson, *Lark Rise to Candleford* (London 1945).

p.145 'dreary and useless'. William Morris, *Hopes and Fears for Art* (London 1882), p. 32.

p.145 'Sit where I like'. *Third Annual Report*.

p.145 Harriet Martineau. Smith, p. 59.

p.146 the simplicity of life'. Morris, p. 32.

p.146 'showed a degree of taste'. *Third Annual Report*.

p.146 In Wales this was a symbol. Geraint Jenkins, *Life and Tradition in Rural Wales* (London 1976), p. 128.

p.147 'The decent cottage'. Enid Gauldie, *Cruel Habitations. A History of Working Class Housing, 1780–1918* (London 1974).

p.148 Each row of cottages. *Our Coal and Our Coalpits by a Traveller Underground* (London 1853), p. 160.

p.148 'provide comfortable'. Henry Roberts, *The Dwellings of the Labouring Classes and Their Construction*, 4th ed. (London 1850).

THE REVEREND ROBERT HAY COATS

Information about the Revd. Coats and his house comes from his obituary in the *Birmingham Post*, 12 May 1956, and from the Glasgow City Museums and Art Galleries.

p.149 'Even a book'. Hermann Muthesius, *The English House* (London 1979), p. 52. Originally published as *Das Englische Haus* (Berlin 1904).

p.150 'the sumptuousness'. Ibid., p. 213.

p.150 'Begin by casting out'. Alastair Service, *Edwardian Architecture* (London 1977), p. 28. Quoting C.F.A. Voysey.

ILLUSTRATION ACKNOWLEDGMENTS

The author and publishers would like to thank the following by whose kind permission the illustrations are reproduced. The pictures on pages 60, 62, 64–6, 68, *71–4*, 77, 90, *91–2*, 93, 96, 112, 114, 116 are reproduced by gracious permission of Her Majesty The Queen. Abbot Hall Art Gallery, Kendal, Cumbria (The John Harden Collection): 10, *17*, 24, 27–8, *30–3*; Ashmolean Museum, Oxford: 46–51, *53–4*; British Museum: 13, 22, 98–102, 145–6, 148; Edward Brooks: 132–3; Central Library, Bristol: 117–18; Christie's, London: 11; John Cornforth: *110*; Walter D'Arcy Hart: *109*; Peter Evans: 16; Mark Girouard: 14; Glasgow Museum and Art Galleries: 150–1; Leeds Central Library: 142; Leeds Record Office: 139; National Monuments Record: 120; National Portrait Gallery: 103; North of England Open Air Museum: 148; RIBA Library: 107; Mary Ryde: 123, 126; Sir John Summerson: 135; Lance Thirkell: *127*; Victoria and Albert Museum, London: *35–6*, *37–44*, 55–6, 58–9, 105, 108, *128*, 129–30, 147, endpapers; Christopher Wood: 2, 78, 81–2, 85, 87, 141. Photographs were taken by A.C.Cooper, P.J.Gates, Christopher Newall, Tony Russell and John Webb. (Figures in italic indicate pages with colour plates.)

INDEX

Figures in *italic* refer to pages on which illustrations occur and to their captions.

159